Seeing CHRIST

To Ines
with her friend
CBS
12/23/93

WINDOWS ON HIS SAVING GRACE

Seeing CHRIST

CALVIN ROCK

REVIEW AND HERALD® PUBLISHING ASSOCIATION
Hagerstown, MD 21740

Texts credited to Amplified are from *The Amplified Bible.* Copyright © 1965 by Zondervan Publishing House. Used by permission.

Texts credited to NIV are from the *Holy Bible, New International Version.* Copyright © 1973, 1978, 1984, International Bible Society. Used by permission of Zondervan Bible Publishers.

Texts credited to NKJV are from The New King James Version. Copyright © 1979, 1980, 1982, Thomas Nelson, Inc., Publishers.

Texts credited to TCNT are from *The Twentieth Century New Testament,* Fleming H. Revell Co., 1900.

Bible texts credited to TEV are from the *Good News Bible*—Old Testament: Copyright © American Bible Society 1976; New Testament: Copyright © American Bible Society 1966, 1971, 1976.

Verses marked TLB are taken from *The Living Bible,* copyright © 1971 by Tyndale House Publishers, Wheaton, Ill. Used by permission.

This book was
Edited by Bill Cleveland
Designed by Ron J. Pride
Inset cover photo by Roger Markham Smith ©Tony Stone Worldwide
Back cover photo by Sam Brown

PRINTED IN U.S.A.

99 98 97 96 95 94   10 9 8 7 6 5 4 3 2 1

R & H Cataloging Service
Rock, Calvin B.
    Seeing Christ: windows on His saving grace.

    1. Jesus Christ—Intercession. 2. Righteousness.
I. Title. II. Title: Windows on His grace.

            232.3

ISBN 0-8280-0794-2

Dedication

This book is dedicated to my grandsons, Anthony, 14; Calvin, 10; John, 7; and David, 7, in the hope that this subject will in the coming years be as precious to them as it is to me.

Acknowledgments

Special thanks for motivation in undertaking this project are due my friend Pastor Neal C. Wilson, who encouraged me to write in this area, and to Phyllis Clendaniel, who was my secretary during most of its development.

CONTENTS

PREFACE

Much is made today of the debates surrounding the nature of Christ and how our ethics and behavior are tied to our stance on that question.

We cannot completely understand the intricacies of the Incarnation, including the question of whether Christ came with Adam's nature before or after the Fall. However, we have sufficient statements in Scripture and subsequent inspiration to suggest both the importance of this subject and the legitimacy of its investigation.

It should be remembered, however, that we are benefited in this regard only when our attempts are to glean understanding of salvation. In other words, the nature of Christ is important to us only as it speaks to and illuminates the grace of Christ.

It is possible to enjoy such dialogue in hundreds of biblical types, 21 of which are explored in this book. It is my belief that this method of reflection provides clarification seldom gleaned in polemical debate.

There is, of course, room in the Christian faith for interpretations other than the one that this volume highlights. This book is not the final answer to those who believe otherwise.

On the other hand, it is, I trust, a clear declaration of the fact that "grace minus nothing, plus nothing" is what saves and that radical dependence upon Christ's righteousness, contrary to what some believe, increases, not decreases, our impulses to obey.

Many who read this volume will experience for the first time an acquaintance with the way in which Ellen G. White assists in Bible study. I believe that your curiosity will be amply rewarded. In this book, many of this author's works are identified; others for purposes of readability are not. Those quotes that are not credited to an author are from her pen.

FOREWORD

One often ponders upon reading a good book what an alternate title might have been. For this timely and provocative little volume, I think I might have suggested something like *Peeps Through the Cosmic Keyhole.* Then again, I'd have to abandon that metaphor, since now in modern times keyholes are not quite "peepable" anymore—thanks to modern security technology. But that's just what this fine little disquisition on the nature, ministry, and meaning of Christ provides—sublime peeks at our wonderful Lord.

But I guarantee that you'll not peek and run, for each of these focused discussions on an aspect of Christ's total submission for us—in every area of human need—will prove irresistible; you'll pause long at each, gazing into each room, soaking up the rich insights stored there. And you will leave stimulated and inspired, pondering the points that have piqued your interest.

You'll discover that this is not a superficial, "once-over-lightly" treatment of the Christ themes, that the book is rich in theological, philosophical, and psychological allusions—and thoroughly bibical. Wide-ranging and reflective study has obviously provided the seedbed for each discussion of the Christ profile. It's apparent that Dr. Rock has earned the right to speak on this subject. And we are all the richer for it.

Twenty-one chapters in all—ideal for three weeks of your daily personal devotions. As Roger Bacon put it so aptly: "Some books are to be just tasted or savored, and some to be digested." This one is definitely in the latter category: one chapter at a time for optimum benefit.

If you've got a three-week vacation or an extended trip in the works, follow the media ad: "Don't leave home without it!"

George Akers

INTRODUCTION

Sooner or later—and the sooner the better—the maturing Christian discovers the blessed truth that our salvation is entirely of Christ and that we overcoming sinners are ever in need of His merciful forgiveness.

This volume reveals how this theme is unfolded in various biblical representations of Christ. But it is more than a rehearsal of struggle and victory in Jesus; it is grateful praise to Him whose holiness is the guarantee of acceptance of all who surrender to His will.

Until we are privileged to stand in His physical presence, we cannot truly understand the mystery of Christ's righteous gift of holiness. Even then the study of His magnanimity will occupy eternity. But we are here and now permitted glimpses of that love through the window of His Word, and by these ever-sharpening visuals of His grace we are motivated to deeper surrender and wider service.

WINDOWS ON
HIS ATTRACTION

CHAPTER I

CHRIST OUR RIGHTEOUS SOUL DESIRE

"Woe is me! for I am as when they have gathered the summer fruits, as the grapegleanings of the vintage: there is no cluster to eat: my soul desired the firstripe fruit" (Micah 7:1).

A "soul desire" is a deep-seated yearning—a thirst so intense and persistent as to be radically disturbing when unfulfilled, and overwhelmingly rewarding when satisfied. Christ is our righteous soul desire.

The longing for communion with the Creator is an enduring quest of society—we humans *will* worship! Often we have done so by mistakenly attributing divinity to other mortals, or to creatures of a lower order, or even to objects of nature. This predisposition to surrender to the most powerful or most wise—or whatever defines for one the "sacred"—has fueled the flames of religion across the centuries. And it is this longing that is fulfilled in knowing Christ.

But how can we truly know the Divine, we without whom the world existed so long and whose soon demise the lengthening years will quickly obscure? We are but integers displayed briefly on the screen of time. Our perceptions are limited by the inferior apparatus of our fallen humanity. What can we really know?

We were not present at Creation, nor did we behold the events in Eden or Bethlehem or Calvary. We must "walk by faith, not by sight" (2 Cor. 5:7). How, then, can we see the Unseen, know the Unknowable?

The answer is, we can't know. We infer, we ascribe, we deduce, we conclude, we believe—but we cannot prove; hence, we do not know.

But Jesus knows!—and we know Him.

Christ is the answer to our quest for meaning.

People of other religious persuasions have responded to the question of life's meaning with various theories of cosmological and cataclysmic import. Buddhists, Hindus, Zoroastrians—all of the great non-Christian religions—claim mystical awareness regarding our origins and our afterlife.

But these theories are not credible to our senses of logic and proportion. We are Christians because the Bible's answers to life's mysteries make more sense than any other "authority."

No, we cannot prove God.

But His Word speaks to us in terms that are wondrous and attractive. Without Him history seems a random hodgepodge of happenstance. With Him history becomes a divinely ordained pattern moving to a happy culmination. Without Him science is an ever-receding study of finite structures. With Him science is the reflection of the divine mind. Without Him life is the result of a random conception followed by a meaningless existence. With Him life is a stage of opportunity, a time of preparation for the world beyond.

As Christians we recognize that life with our Saviour is not a period of uninterrupted joy. Tragedy, failure, disappointment, pain, and death befall us all.

But in this dark existence His Word enlightens us—His promises are true, and His predictions are unerring. We are attracted by His life. His Holy Spirit empowers us. We are diseased but determined, devalued by sin but revalued in Him, dying but hopeful. We do not slake our thirst with mind-depressing drugs or energy-arousing stimulants.

Because we have found meaning in Him, we see, through faith's eyes, the land of promise and take hope. Jesus is enough.

Christ is the answer to our desire for forgiveness.

Not only do we thirst for meaning; we long for forgiveness, for relief from guilt and culpability.

There are many sources to which humans turn for such freedom. No one who has visited the Buddhist pagodas in the Far East can ever forget the sight of worshipers laying gifts at Buddha's feet, in Buddha's lap, on Buddha's tongue. They burn their incense with bowed heads and clasped hands, praying for help from the "enlightened one." But the statue of Buddha does not offer forgiveness or freedom from culpability. Buddha cannot hear, and his followers, relieved of their offerings but not of their sins, must finally scrape their rotting sacrifices from the stony presence of their unblinking god. Their emotions are assuaged, but their transgressions remain—and so does their guilt.

But are they any different from the long train of misguided petitioners who from the ill-conceived sacrifice of Cain to this day have offered to gods of wood and stone? Not only have people sacrificed the fruit of their hands but also that of their wombs—their children as well as their elderly, their enemies, and even themselves in bloody attempts to appease and/or gratify their gods.

But gods that cannot hear cannot forgive. Gods that cannot breathe cannot bless. Gods that cannot speak cannot communicate acceptance. Gods that cannot create cannot re-create.

Only a living God—an incarnated, crucified, and resurrected Saviour—can plead our cause before the Father and undo our sordid past. Only a victorious, living Lord can nullify our transgressions.

Christ is the answer to our need for moral certainty.

We humans cannot help but sense the chasm that exists between what we are and what we should be—the suspicion that we are being judged by a standard higher than ourselves weighs heavily upon our consciences. Jesus is the answer to that universal phenomenon.

There are, of course, many avenues traveled in the search for morality. Theories grounded in nature, culture, intuition, science, and philosophy have rivaled godliness since the Fall.

But none of the above yields an acceptable ethic. Why? Because every moral theory requires, with description, the "transcendence of prescription," thereby mandating a superior intelligence. Every ethic is grounded in some ultimate source, and since there is only one great "I AM," all ethical theories that are not grounded in His Word lack final authority. Because of its relation to Christ, the absolute being, Christian ethics is the absolute morality.

The tenents of Christian ethics are absolute because its Source is absolute, because its "integrating center" is Jesus Christ, the only teacher whose life completely equaled his or her ideal construct.

Christian ethics rejects the theory that the "oughtness" of morality can be derived from the "isness" of consequence, or of might, or even from nature. Instead, it demands that we chart our way through the maze of daily decision-making by studying and applying the principles of the Word of God.

To know Christ is to know life eternal, to live life at its best—to have within us "wells of living water" that alone can quench our desire for morality.

Christ is the answer to our search for happiness.

The quest for happiness has been the primary subject of moral philosophers and political orators down through time. Well-intentioned theorists have stressed the need for peace, justice, temperance, and a number of other virtues as antidotes for human problems. But most often expressed is the need for happiness.

The philosopher Aristotle identified happiness as "an activity of the soul in accordance with perfect virtue," the primary aim and highest good of humanity (Richard McKeon, ed., *Basic Works of Aristotle*, p. 1095a).

Immanuel Kant, seeking to improve upon that definition, connected happiness not with virtuous states, but to law and duty. That is because he viewed the diversity and differences inherent in definitions of virtue as unstable anchors for happiness.

But these and all other such theories are hopelessly flawed because they make happiness a goal instead of a consequence—the chief objective of life rather than the by-product of a relationship with Jesus Christ.

If happiness, as we believe, is the result of fellowship with Christ, why, then, are the "Christian nations" of today so unhappy, so unhealthy, so burdened with mental, physical, and social disease? It is because God's promises are conditional. He doesn't bless our vows; He blesses our obedience. The moral decay of nations that claim His name is a result of their unwillingness, professions of pious intent notwithstanding, to do His will.

The moral deprivation suffered by so-called Christian nations is stark proof of the validity of the principle that states: "Righteousness exalteth a nation: but sin is a reproach to any people" (Prov. 14:34).

People who seek happiness in the vain, *thing*ified societies of this generation are doomed to disappointment. Sadly, their epitaph is the verdict spoken long ago to those persons who sought Him out among the tombs—"He is not here."

Christ is the answer to our longing for peace.

Augustine gave earnest expression to the search for peace when, conscience-smitten and repentant, he prayed: "Man is one of Your creatures, Lord, and his instinct is to praise You. He bears about him the mark of death, the sign of his own sin, to remind him that You thwart the proud. But still, since he is a part of Your creation, he wishes to praise You. The thought of You stirs him so deeply that he cannot be content unless he praises You, because You made us for Yourself and our hearts find no peace until they rest in You" *(Confessions,* p. 21).

Of what, then, does peace consist? It consists of total faith and trust in Christ, a radical reliance upon His merits, the confidence that His efforts in our behalf are more than sufficient for our reconciliation with God. That is the meaning of Paul's encouraging words:

"Therefore being justified by faith, we have peace with God through our Lord Jesus Christ: by whom also we have access by faith into this grace wherein we stand, and rejoice in hope of the glory of God" (Rom. 5:1, 2).

That is our hardest lesson.

As surely as we have an inborn longing for peace, so surely do we possess a natural perversity that drives us to seek that peace by works and sacrifice. It is seen in the bloody rituals of the pagan and in the practice of the Christian that is no less misguided—one's offering of works, even good works, to earn God's favor and assuage His wrath.

There is, of course, a place for works in the Christian experience. But our works do not curry favor or pardon or peace. Peace, complete and final, is ours when we discover and accept that the impossible debt has been paid, that the impossible life has been lived, and that His blood has been appropriated on our behalf.

Ellen White was correct when she wrote: "It is peace that you need—Heaven's forgiveness and peace and love in the soul. Money cannot buy it, intellect cannot procure it, wisdom cannot attain to it; you can never hope, by your own efforts, to secure it. But God offers it to you as a gift, 'without money and without price'" *(Steps to Christ,* p. 49).

Isaiah understood that truth and expressed it in one of Scripture's most lyrical praises: "I will greatly rejoice in the Lord, my soul shall be joyful in my God; for he hath covered me with the garments of salvation, he hath covered me with the robe of righteousness" (Isa. 61:10).

Christ is our righteous soul desire.

CHAPTER 2

CHRIST OUR RIGHTEOUS SONG OF LOVE

"Behold, thou art fair, my love; behold, thou art fair; thou hast doves' eyes within thy locks: thy hair is as a flock of goats, that appear from mount Gilead. . . . Thou art all fair, my love; there is no spot in thee" (S. of Sol. 4:1-7).

A "song of love" is an expression of desire and surrender, an outpouring of emotion that has as its theme the object of one's abiding affections. Jesus is our righteous song of love.

When we contemplate His goodness, we cannot help but praise His power, marvel at His mercy. Like Solomon, we extol our Beloved for His strength and virtuous beauty, for His tender affection and constant regard.

Christ has numbered the hairs of our head (Matt. 10:30), recorded our tears in a bottle (Ps. 56:8); we are the apple of His eye (Zech. 2:8). He who marks the sparrow's fall and clothes the earth with grass, who provides for His creatures according to their order, knows our every need.

As a father loves to delight his children, so Christ loves to give us good gifts. He delights to shower us with good things (Matt. 7:11). He loved us with an everlasting love (Jer. 31:3).

By Adam's sin and ours we are made ineligible for these benefits, but we are recipients nonetheless. He found a way to rescue us from just and unavoidable destruction.

How can we begin to understand such affection? The vastness of His love surpasses our imagination. We see it, we believe it, but we cannot comprehend it. No language can aptly explain it. Frustrated in our attempts to adequately describe His mercy, we cry in resignation with the awestruck apostle: "Behold, what manner of love the Father hath bestowed upon us" (1 John 3:1)!

How great is the love of Christ? So great that He risked His place in the heavens to save us, so great that He left the imperial majesty of His eternal throne to dwell with us, to live and die in our midst.

To die? Yes, to die in the person of a Man named Jesus Christ. That is the greatest demonstration of His love.

His love was shown in the departure from His throne, in His humble birth, in His life and poverty, in His sacrificial labors, and in His calm restraint under suffering and abuse. But most of all, in the life He gave for us all.

Christ loves us individually and collectively, personally and corporately. He loves us "one-on-one," and He loves us "en masse." To understand how He could love us so is to inquire of the unexplainable mystery of godliness, the inexplicable secret of divine magnanimity.

We cannot understand why—but we know that He does.

Christ's love seeks no advantage, withholds no benefits, demands no favors. It focuses only upon His creature's good and His Father's will. It is higher than the heavens and stronger than death.

Solomon had this quality of love in mind when he wrote: "Many waters cannot quench love, neither can the floods drown it: if a man would give all the substance of his house for love, it would utterly be contemned" (S. of Sol. 8:7).

We extol Christ because He pursued us.

He loved us *before* we loved Him. He sought us. He wooed us by the ministry of His Holy Spirit.

Christ set traps of grace—experiences and circumstances—to gain our attention and stimulate our desire. He afflicted us; He uplifted us. He deflated us; He prospered us. He sent preachers and teachers, tracts and sermons, poetry and prose. He wrote His love in the sky and signaled it on the wings of song. He thundered His love in the tempest and whispered it in the still, small voice at the midnight hour.

In the guilt-ridden aftermath of our transgressions, He prodded our thoughts and aroused our curiosity with blessings we neither expected nor deserved. He sent winds that chilled and zephyrs that refreshed.

Even when we were riveted in our iniquity and refused to hear, He sought us relentlessly. He followed us to danger's door and waited for us to exit. He pursued us over the rough hills of our youthful escapades. He overshadowed us in the dark alleys of lust and doubt. He never gave up. He was patient and persistent, and He was victorious.

He initiated the contact. He made the first move in our relationship, and the second, and all the other steps required to gain our attention.

And then we saw Him. From our deathbeds of sin we saw Him high and lifted up. Some of us responded immediately; like the thief upon the cross, we surrendered quickly and completely. But for most of us the focus was dim at first—we saw Him, but we did not recognize Him. We did not, could not, fully yield.

But He kept calling and sending and pursuing, and finally the fog of worldliness cleared away and we saw Jesus, blessed Jesus, Son of God and Son of man, heaven's richest treasure, dying for the dregs of the universe—for us! *Absolutely incomprehensible?* Yes. But we saw it. We heard it. We felt it. We accepted it.

We fell in love with Jesus. And that reality redirected our priorities and altered our perceptions—all our yesterdays, our todays, and our tomorrows were made new by His love. He is our righteous song of love.

We extol Christ because He purchased us.

Our response is not the payment whereby we are released from the encumbrances of sin. The price of our freedom, the sum that frees us from death's cold grip is the blood of Christ. By His sacrifice we are ransomed. His right to claim us—and our right of release from sin and its consequences—is His dowry of suffering. His blood bought our deliverance.

This grace that we experience—this grace that purchased us, that breaks our hearts and binds our affections to Him—is not of small value. Absolutely not. It is not "cheap grace." It is priceless. Never was there a dowry like this. A million cows or a billion dollars, the world itself, the whole of the universe, cannot equal the life of the Son of God. All things created are replaceable—but not the Creator. Were the heavens, the earth, and all its creatures to suddenly disappear, He would need but speak again, and it would again be done.

Nevertheless, He made Himself vulnerable—for us! The irreplaceable God became a vulnerable human being in order that expendable human beings might regain conditional immortality.

We are bought with a price far greater than the total of all that our senses can comprehend. He is our righteous song of love.

We extol Christ because He prepares us.

The perfect Groom demands a perfect bride, a "glorious church, . . . holy and without blemish" (Eph. 5:27)?

But how can that happen? Our excesses and omissions are obvious. Our daily failures lead us to constantly access the promise: "If we confess our sins, he is faithful and just to forgive us our sins, and to cleanse us from all unrighteousness" (1 John 1:9).

We are no better than the struggling, "not-yet-fully-grown" saints who preceded us in faith. We mirror their states. We are like Isaiah, who confessed: "I am undone; because I am a man of unclean lips" (Isa. 6:5). We resemble Paul, who proclaimed himself the chief of sinners (1 Tim. 1:15). How can this generation of believers possibly claim to be better than they? How can we, His church, His bride, claim readiness for our marriage with the Lamb? That is, without spot or wrinkle or any such thing?

The beloved apostle provided the answer in his charge: "Be glad and rejoice, and give honor to him: for the marriage of the Lamb is come, and his wife hath made herself ready. And to her was granted that she should be arrayed in fine linen, clean and white: for the fine linen is the righteousness of saints" (Rev. 19:7, 8).

Christ's robe of righteousness, the "fine linen, clean and white," makes us ready, not our goodness. His covering, not our achieving, provides the absolute purity required of the bride. And that is why Paul can speak of us as a "radiant church, without stain or wrinkle or any other blemish, but holy and blameless" (Eph. 5:27, NIV).

To Paul the believers were saints: the feuding members at Rome were saints (Rom. 1:7); the worldly Christians at Jerusalem were saints (Rom. 12:13); the often-confused members at Corinth were saints (1 Cor. 14:33; 2 Cor. 1:1); the bickering members at Ephesus were saints (Eph. 1:1); the materialistic congregation at Philippi were saints (Phil. 1:1); the believers at Colossae who were given to vain disputes were nonetheless saints (Col. 1:2).

And we today are saints.

But clearly, being a saint is not enough. Saints are still wrestling, still growing, still overcoming—saints are sinners saved by grace. But to them is granted the qualifying robe of preparation: the immaculate life of Christ's righteousness. Thus, we respond to the wisdom that pleads:

> "You have your work clothes on, my Dear,
> That simply will not do.
> The Wedding's near. Please will you wear
> The garments bought for you!"
> (Jane W. Lauber).

We extol Christ because He forgives us.

The truth is, even after discovering His Love, after entrusting ourselves into His care, after experiencing our newfound happiness, we are not always faithful. We sin. We disappoint Him. We break our vows. We go back on our promises.

And He knows. He forgives as the father forgave the prodigal son, as Hosea forgave His profligate wife. He does not revoke the contract. He does not cast us out or write us off. He does not evict or excommunicate us. He lovingly forgives.

Christ, whose name is Faithful and True, never breaks faith; He keeps His pledge without deviation or diminution. He remains faithful to us who are so often unfaithful to Him. We who are so severe with our children and with each other, we whose petty grudges rankle and fester in our proud hearts, are shamed as we experience that forgiveness. And we are inspired to forgive one another.

How have we shamed Him?

We shame Him with our selfishness, our tribalism, our lethargy; with our materialism, our excesses of appetite, work, and pleasure. We shame Him by watching others suffer without response. By being content to live sumptuously while others struggle in poverty. By withdrawing our churches from the crowded thoroughfares, never to return. By being silent while evil men and women misuse their powers and rule intemperately.

The love that He gives us in spite of our ill-suitedness rings out in Robert Herrick's words:

> "God's boundless mercy is to sinful man
> Like to the ever-wealthy ocean;
> Which, though it sends forth thousand streams, 'tis ne'er
> Known, or else seen, to be emptier:
> And though it takes all in, 'tis yet no more
> Full and filled full than when fulfilled before"
> *(The Pulpit Commentary,* vol. 32, p. 104).

But we must not think His forgiveness is an excuse for disobedience. He who said "Rise, take up thy bed, and walk" (John 5:8) also commanded, "Go, and sin no more" (John 8:11). The disciple who recorded these words wrote: "Little children, these things write I unto you, that ye sin not" (1 John 2:1). But happily, he added: "If any man sin, we have an advocate with the Father, Jesus Christ the righteous" (verse 2).

He is our advocate, our brother, our never-failing guide.

Ellen G. White made known her confidence: "I know that He loves me, notwithstanding my imperfection. I rest in His love. God has accepted His perfection in my behalf. He is my righteousness, and I trust in His merits" *(Signs of the Times,* Aug. 13, 1902).

He loves us, He pursues us, He purchases us, He prepares us, He forgives us, and He claims us as His bride. There is no greater love, no deeper mystery, no higher joy—no richer sacrifice.

Christ is our righteous song of love.

CHAPTER 3

CHRIST OUR RIGHTEOUS STAR OF HOPE

"I Jesus have sent mine angel to testify unto you these things in the churches. I am the root and the offspring of David, and the bright and morning star" (Rev. 22:16).

The "morning star" is the brightest sentinel of the night sky. But it is more than just an object of aesthetic wonder; it functions in dependable practicality, bringing direction, confidence, and assurance to the human race. Christ is our righteous star of hope.

Consider the many ways the morning star mirrors the ministry of our Lord.

The location of the morning star provides sure direction.

People of the distant past depended upon the stars for guidance. They were largely obligated to astronomical patterns for both seasonal and directional guidance. For most of earth's millenniums, crusaders and commoners were led in their conquests by the starry patterns of night.

Today's sophisticated radios, computers, and radar have taken us far beyond their simple tools, allowing us to traverse the earth—and even sortie into space—supremely confident of our routes and destinations. But our fascination with the stars remains.

Jesus is our guiding star. To the Christian He is the source of unerring direction. He guides us by His Word. In all matters and manner of decision, the Bible points the way.

He who made both us and the world we inhabit knows what is best. He knows our strengths and our infirmities. He promises that when we need guidance, we "shall hear a word . . . saying, This is the way, walk ye in it" (Isa. 30:21). And to ensure our eternal benefit, He pledged: "I will pray the Father, and he shall give you another Comforter, that he may abide with you for ever" (John 14:16). We are not alone.

He is generous in this guidance. Not only does He answer our pleas for direction in those projects that we hold up in prayer; He precedes us through dangers of which we are not aware. And although there are times when He guides us to circumstances that bring hardship and pain, we are comforted when we remember that "God never leads His children otherwise than they would choose to be led, if they could see the end from the beginning" *(The Ministry of Healing,* p. 479).

The closer we conform to His laws, the clearer is His voice in our hearts. It is when we stray from the path of His leading that His instructions grow dim, that we are overcome with our challenges. It is when we forget to pray that we trace with less accuracy His plan for our lives. It is when, emboldened by prior excursions into sin, we go heedlessly onto Satan's ground that we are trapped by temptation. It is when, like Peter, we turn our eyes away from Him to display our own spiritual levitation that we sink beneath the waves of sin.

His directions give us compass; His instructions bring us safety. We beam in upon Him, and He guides us from the lowlands of sin to the highlands of salvation where we are safe in the Father's care.

The dependability of the morning star provides us moral courage.

The morning star is always there. Even when obscured to human eyes, its orbit and place are predictable. Jesus is always there—an ever-present help in the time of trouble.

We would despair utterly were it were not for Him. His dependability is the anchor of our faith. His loving characteristics do not change.

Augustine expressed this certainty when he wrote: "Anything, if it is changeable, . . . does not truly exist; for there is not true existence wherever nonexistence has a place. Sift through mutations of things, thou wilt find 'was' and 'will be.' Think on God; thou wilt find is where 'was' and will be cannot exist" (Robert Jordan, "Time and Contingency in Saint Augustine," in R. A. Markus, ed., *Augustine: A Collection of Essays,* p. 270).

More certain than our growth in wisdom is our regress toward death. Even in the midst of our joys, we see the harbingers of our mortality. No sooner are we born than we begin to die. The aging of our organs, the leakage of our vitality, the decay of the "outer man," the "tabernacle" that clothes us (2 Cor. 5:4), highlights the sureness of our doom.

Death is the final change. It reconfigures our family circles and reconstructs our societies. One by one, people we know are removed from the table of our youth—family and friends we held dear and whose company we still crave.

Time rearranges our associations. The years rob us of people with whom we once shared happy confidences and pristine joys. New challenges and directives have structured for them increasingly divergent patterns of living. Often we look up from the confusion of our jangled lives for the smile of that person we once enjoyed, and it is not there. We are constantly forced to adjust, often with flayed emotions, sagging confidences, and a reduced capacity to face life with optimism.

But Jesus is always there. He never forsakes us. We know where to look. And when we turn to Him, we find Him ever present, ever faithful, ever true. "I am the Lord," He reassures us, "I change not" (Mal. 3:6).

The nearness of the morning star provides us temporal meaning.

What we call the morning star is actually a planet—its name is Venus. And because it is similar in size and revolves closer to earth than any other planet, it is known as the "twin sister" of our world. Because of its astronomical proximity, Venus is both our morning and evening star. When seen in the western sky, it is the evening star, labeled *Hesperus* by the Greeks. And when visible in the east, it is the morning star, or *Phosphorus,* as they called it—meaning "light bearing," or that which glows in darkness.

Jesus is our morning star. He is our nearest of kin, our "friend that sticketh closer than a brother" (Prov. 18:24). He is Emmanuel—"God with us" (Matt. 1:23). He "tabernacled" with us, and "we beheld his glory, the glory as of the only begotten of the Father, full of grace and truth (John 1:14). The Centerpiece of heaven became the central event of human history; around Him rotates all our chronology and meaning. By His life, we separate time into B.C. and A.D., we divide the Old Testament and the New. He is the fulfillment of the old covenant and the promise of the new.

He challenged the uncontested reign of the kingdom of darkness and ushered in the all-conquering rule of the kingdom of light. He ended the free fall of humanity that began in Eden and led the revival of human intellect that began at Bethlehem. By His life, we distinguish *kairos* from *chronos* and redefine time as "the space between the eternities."

The beauty of the morning star provides us aesthetic wonder.

The stars are beautiful. The silver garlands that sparkle in the darkened night are unrivaled in luster. That person who has not stood in awe beneath their shimmering glory lacks life's surest proof that "a thing of beauty is a joy forever." So great is the aesthetic impact of these heavenly orbs upon our senses that we find no higher compliment than to label as "stars" the most attractive and gifted among us.

And there are myriads of stars to contemplate. In prior decades many astronomers considered our galaxy of more than 100 billion stars to be unique—that it was *the* universe. But the giant telescopes through which we now peer reveal that there are literally millions of other galaxies, each with its own numberless complement of stars. So densely populated are these island universes that they seem as mist or swirling clouds on a moonlit night.

The nearest stars to earth, Proxima Centauri and Alpha Centauri, are about 270 trillion miles away. Moving at the speed of light—an astounding rate of 11 million miles a minute!—the illumination emitted by these stars takes 4.3 years to reach the earth. The spiral nebula M 51, in the constellation Canes Venatici, is 50 light years away, an "average" distance. And the most distant known object of all, a quasar discovered by the Anglo-Australian observatory in Australia, is 13.8 billion light years from earth.

The stars exhibit some amazing characteristics. Delta Cephei, for example, is a pulsating star. Betelgeuse, with a diameter some 460 times that of our sun, is so immense that it would swallow up the orbits of the inner planets of our solar system. Vega appears blue-white in color, and Antares almost ruby red. Cappella has an apparent motion away from the earth of about 1 million miles a day. Spica is seen in this hemisphere mainly in the spring. Also in the great canopy above are supernovas—catastrophically exploding stars.

But to us there is no star like the morning star. It is the star that charms us most. It is the star that we see when all others are dimmed by atmospheric conditions or earth's orbital tilt. It is the brightest of the heavenly bodies except for the sun and the moon.

Jesus is our bright morning star, more lustrous, more versatile, more scintillating, more functional, than any other. Many other beacons point us to God: nature declares His glory, history traces His wisdom, human intuition—though skewed by sin—perceives His reality. Jesus is the primary revelation, the chief indicator of His Father's being.

When He came to this earth, it was our worst hour. Darkness covered the earth, and "gross darkness the people" (Isa. 60:2). People had locked themselves in the paralyzing vise of idolatry and baleful pagan practices. Steeped in superstition, mired in tradition, charmed by the fanciful imaginations of Greek and Roman mythology that exalted nonbeings into creator-deities, the population of earth suffered the darkness of moral night.

It was upon this woeful scene that there shone "a Star out of Jacob" (Num. 24:17) and those who "walked in darkness" beheld "a great light" (Isa. 9:2). Hopeless humanity heard His words and said, "Never man spake like this man" (John 7:46). Witnessing His humility, they cried, "Truly this was the Son of

God" (Matt. 27:54). Recounting His sayings, they concluded, "Did not our heart burn within us, while he talked with us by the way, and while he opened to us the scriptures?" (Luke 24:32).

But the masses refused to accept Him.

He was a light shining in the darkness, but "the darkness comprehended it not" (John 1:5). Evil sought to overwhelm and extinguish Him. And He was indeed eclipsed from our view for a portion of three days.

But the Star that rose from Jacob's lineage also rose from Joseph's tomb. He sank briefly from our view only to arise with His luster increased. And He is shining still. He shines when all other hope has been clouded by time and eroded by circumstance. We have discovered that He is "all that is real . . . and such beginnings as shall eternally develop and never contract into fixity and decline" *(The Biblical Illustrator,* vol. 23, p. 755).

Christ's righteous life gives luster to His being. His selfless condescension, His merciful healing, His sympathy for the underclass—the poor, the outcasts— and His resistance to evil reveal a love unequaled in time. His life stands out above all others because He did what no other has done: He lived a flawless existence—and now He heightens our wonder and exceeds our comprehension by sharing His marvelous victory with feeble sinners.

His character is beautiful, not just in His heavenly preexistence; He was all God then. But in His earthly experience, the one He forged in human garb. He, our star, is beautiful in the unfolding of prophecy, beautiful in His revelation of principle, and beautiful in His fulfillment of His promises to His people.

Christ is shining still—He is "no mere name of tender recollection, no dear relic of a perished past, to be drawn sometimes in silence from its casket and clasped with the aching fondness and sprinkled with the hot tears of hopeless memory. He is not Hesperus that sets, but phosphorus that rises, springing into the sky through the earliest dawn; the pledge of reviving life, and growing light, and all the energies and all the pleasures of the happy day" *(ibid.).*

We mortals are still under the bondage of the fleshly laws that decree our certain demise. Where sin abides, death reigns; and where death reigns, darkness remains. We long for the dawning of that bright world where there will be no night, where iniquity shall not rise the second time, where time shall lapse into eternity, where the Lamb is the eternal light.

Meanwhile, we take hope, knowing that "weeping may endure for a night, but joy cometh in the morning" (Ps. 30:5). The surest sign of the coming dawn is the singular radiance of His appearance.

Christ is our righteous morning star.

Windows on His Presence

CHAPTER 4

CHRIST OUR RIGHTEOUS SHEWBREAD

"And upon the table of shewbread they shall spread a cloth of blue, and put thereon the dishes, and the spoons, and the bowls, and covers to cover withal: and the continual bread shall be thereon"
(Num. 4:7)

The shewbread consisted of 12 cakes, or loaves, neatly arranged on a table that stood in the north corner of the holy place of the Hebrew sanctuary. Referred to as the "bread of presence," it was *never* absent from its place in the ritual service. Christ is our righteous shewbread.

In the sanctuary ritual there were two major types of sacrifices: the burnt offerings and the meal offerings, referred to in Scripture as "meat offerings" (Lev. 2:1-3). The burnt offerings symbolized personal surrender—by them the offerer said, "All that I *am* is the Lord's." The meal offerings symbolized sacrificial giving—by them the offerer said, "All that I *have* is the Lord's." The shewbread was a meal offering.

Each of the 12 loaves was made of four fifths of a peck of fine flour. The shewbread was arranged in two stacks of six loaves, both stacks sprinkled with incense, with a cup of incense on top.

The table that held the shewbread was called the "pure table" (Lev. 24:6). It was made of shittim wood and overlaid with gold. In addition to the shewbread, the table had on it "dishes, and the spoons, and the bowls, and covers to cover withal" (Num. 4:7).

The bread was changed each Sabbath (Lev. 24:8), when as the outgoing priests finished their week of service they removed the old bread, and the incoming priests put fresh loaves in its place.

Our understanding and appreciation for Christ's ministry is illustrated and enhanced by each of the symbols contained in the shewbread arrangement. Following are certain elements that are especially helpful to our spiritual insight.

The table of shewbread was constructed from shittim wood.

Shittim (acacia) wood is exceptionally strong and durable. So dense as to be virtually impenetrable, shittim wood is resistant to decay, attack by insects, and the ravages of time, qualities that made it ideal for long years of reliable use. It was also aromatic.

The durable nature of shittim wood is an arresting symbol of our reliable Saviour. His victory over sin gives lasting hope to struggling humanity. His death for sinners is a perpetual fragrance before the Father's throne.

The table was overlaid with gold.

Sometimes called the "pure table," the table of shewbread was not only substantially strong and aromatically fragrant; it was aesthetically attractive with its polished gold covering (Ex. 25:11).

Jesus is our beautiful Saviour. He is distinguished by appearance as well as by substance, by words as well as deeds, by philosophy as well as action. How beautiful is He? He is fairer than the morning; constellations pale in comparison.

In the garden of His passion His visage was terribly marred, His noble form was bruised and cut by whip and rod, by painful thorns and blows. But this is how He became the loveliest of us all. That is what we mean when we sing the words of the "crusader hymn":

> "Fairest Lord Jesus,
>   Ruler of all nature,
>   O Thou of God and man the Son!
>   Thee will I cherish,
>   Thee will I honor,
>   Thou art my glory, joy, and crown.
>
> Fair are the meadows,
>   Fairer still the woodlands,
>   Robed in the blooming garb of spring;
>   Jesus is fairer,
>   Jesus is purer,
>   Who makes the woeful heart to sing."

The table of shewbread was covered with a cloth of blue.

The brilliant gold of the shewbread table was muted by a blue cloth (Num. 4:11). In Old Testament times the colors blue and scarlet were actually two shades of purple. Those materials in which red dominated were called scarlet crimson. When blue prevailed, it was labeled blue, or violet, and was less stunning—therefore, more palatable to the eye.

Jesus is the "softened presence" of God among us. Had He come in all His blazing glory, we could not have survived His brightness. He "stepped down" His glory, dimmed His radiance, so He could "tabernacle" among us.

The table of shewbread contained bowls, or flagons.

Drink offerings often accompanied the meal offerings of the sanctuary (Lev. 23:13). Whereas burnt offerings commemorated dedication and meal offerings commemorated sacrifice, drink offerings represented happiness or refreshing. Jesus is the fount of all our joy and rejoicing.

Christ poured out His blood before God as a "drink offering" on our behalf. The good news of our redemption relieves our anxieties and brings glad anticipation of the time when He will drink the cup with us in the earth made new (Luke 22:18).

There were 12 loaves of bread.

The number 12 testifies to divine appointment, of having been chosen. There were 12 sons of Jacob, whose descendants comprised the 12 tribes of Israel. There were 12 stones taken from the bed of the Jordan commemorating Israel's deliverance from Egypt and its birth as a nation. There were 12 disciples chosen as the original proponents of the kingdom of His grace. There are 12 foundations to the New Jerusalem, upon which sit 12 gates through which will pass the faithful of the earth.

Jesus is the Father's "chosen," His "twelve," His anointed instrument of salvation. "This is my beloved Son," the Father declares, "in whom I am well pleased" (Matt. 3:17). By His life we are both chosen and fitted for everlasting life.

The bread was made of fine flour.

Flour is milled grain. In Bible days it was ground or beaten to a coarse meal. While on the stalk, the grain is itself a living thing—it contains the spark of life. When made into flour, the grain becomes food, life for other creatures.

Jesus is our grain, our fine flour. He was beaten and bruised and ground beneath the wheels of injustice. He was crushed in order that we might live. He was rendered lifeless that we might live again. His death makes His life efficacious to us.

The bread was sprinkled with frankincense.

Frankincense is very costly. More so than myrrh and other more common types of incense. When burned, it produced an aromatic cloud that sweetened the priestly offering.

Jesus is our fragrant presence before the Father. The participation of Christ in our communion with God is a critical element in making our prayers acceptable. The consequences of His obedience "unto death" is a fragrance that provides our stammering expressions with coherence and value and effectiveness.

There was no time when the shewbread was not present.

The priests who were on duty for the ensuing week began their service at the Friday-evening sacrifice—the beginning of God's holy day. The priests whom they were to relieve remained with them until the Sabbath-morning sacrifice. At its completion, the outgoing priests removed the old loaves while the incoming priests brought in new loaves, freshly baked. There was no hiatus, no gap, no time at which the bread was not in place.

Thus, the shewbread was the bread of the presence, "the continual bread" (Num. 4:7), an "ever-present testimony that Israel was dependent upon God for sustenance and a constant promise from God that He would sustain them. Their need was ever before Him and His promise constantly before them" (M. L. Andreason, *The Sanctuary Service,* p. 106).

Jesus is our continual sustainer before the Father. He neither sleeps nor slumbers. There is no time when He is not present. In Hebrews 7:25 we are assured that He "ever liveth to make intercession for" us.

The shewbread was eaten.

The bread was consumed by the priests, who, as representatives of the people, petitioned God on their behalf. Bread on the table may be appetizing and attractive—but bread internalized is the only kind that brings strength.

Jesus is our shewbread, and since we are now a nation of priests, a "holy priesthood" (1 Peter 2:5), we must appropriate Him for ourselves. He must be daily consumed in the study of His Word if we would be energized by His presence. When we concentrate upon the Word of God, we assimilate His principles, we absorb His love, we partake of the nutrients of His words.

Jesus is the staff of life, the strength whereby we function, our source of inspiration and energy, the daily fount of power whereby we overcome and maintain in the spiritual warfare.

The bread was mixed with oil.

In the Scriptures, oil represents the Holy Spirit, "blessed third" of the Trinity.

He was promised and sent by Christ to "reprove the world of sin, and of righteousness, and of judgment" (John 16:8), to guide His people "into all truth" (verse 13).

The Holy Spirit is as great and as good as Christ. In the work of redemption He utilizes His influence to glorify Christ, who joins with Him in glorifying God the Father.

Present but indistinguishable in the sanctuary loaves is the Holy Spirit, who, though unseen, is distinctly and powerfully present in our individual lives and the life of the corporate Christian church. He brings us conviction regarding Christ. He illumines our studies, inspires our zeal, directs our faith, prospers our labors.

When with us, Jesus spoke many "I am's," each of which is a dynamic illustration of His love for us and the relationship that we must sustain for victory and acceptance with the Father. "I am the light of the world," He said (John 8:12). "I am the way, the truth, and the life" (John 14:6); "I am the true vine" (John 15:1); "I am the resurrection, and the life" (John 11:25); "I am the good shepherd" (John 10:14).

But none is more essential than His assertion: "I am the bread of life" (John 6:35).

His Word is our source of regeneration and growth. We are born again by His Word, we grow by His Word, we are led to repentance by His Word, we are sanctified by His Word, we are sustained by His Word, we are warned by His Word, we are taught by His Word, we are saved by His Word. No wonder the psalmist exclaimed: "O taste and see that the Lord is good" (Ps. 34:8). No wonder Jeremiah could say: "Thy words were found, and I did eat them; and thy word was unto me the joy and rejoicing of my heart" (Jer. 15:16).

Our need of God's Word is no more appropriately expressed than in Mary A. Lathbury's hymn:

> "Break Thou the bread of life, Dear Lord, to me,
>   As Thou didst break the loaves Beside the sea;
>   Beyond the sacred page, I seek thee, Lord;
>   My spirit pants for Thee, O living Word. . . .
>
> Spirit and life are they, Words Thou dost speak;
>   I hasten to obey, But I am weak;
>   Thou art my only help, Thou art my life;
>   Heeding Thy holy Word I win the strife."

Christ is our righteous shewbread.

CHAPTER 5

CHRIST OUR RIGHTEOUS SOVEREIGN

"My mouth will tell of your righteousness, of your salvation all day long, though I know not its measure. I will come and proclaim your mighty acts, O Sovereign Lord; I will proclaim your righteousness, yours alone" (Ps. 71:15, 16, NIV).

A sovereign is one who exercises absolute rule in the lives of others. The sovereign has no peers and does not share authority. He or she alone controls. Subjects are people who live under the rule of a sovereign; they surrender to the sovereign their total homage and obedience. Christ is our righteous sovereign.

Christ is our Creator-Sovereign.

The Scriptures identify Christ as the focal point of Creation. "He [Christ] spake, and it was done; he commanded, and it stood fast," explained the psalmist (Ps. 33:9). "By Him all things were created that are in heaven and that are on earth. . . . All things were created through Him and for Him," Paul added, speaking of Christ (Col. 1:16, NKJV).

Our Lord has existed from eternity. He was with God the Father in the "unbegun beginning." He is the righteous Son of God, the embodiment of the Father, the only begotten, the great I AM, to whom angels owe their creation and for which they give Him glory and joyful service.

We humans also praise His creative power.

We praise Him not simply because it is greater than our comprehension, but because what little we do understand is so wondrous in form and in function. We praise His creatorship because its dynamics elude our understanding, because its manifestations stagger our imagination and delight our senses.

When we behold the stars, the moon, the work of His hands, we cry out with David, "O Lord, our Lord, how majestic is your name in all the earth!" (Ps. 8:1, NIV).

Impacted by the beauty and enormity of nature, the wondering creature is made to confess:

"I understand that matter can be changed
To energy; that maths can integrate
The complex quantum jumps that must relate
The fusion of the stars to history's page.
I understand that God in every age
Is Lord of all; that matter can't dictate;
That stars and quarks and all things intricate
Perform His word—including fool and sage.

But knowing God is not to know like God;
And science is a quest in infancy.
Still more: transcendence took on flesh and blood:
I do not understand how this can be.
The more my mind is stretched to understand,
The more it learns the finitude of man"
(D. A. Carson).

Christ is our Redeemer-Sovereign.

"Transcendence took on flesh and blood!" That is the most glorious thought of all. We are awed by the exalted attributes of One who is "righteous in all his ways" (Ps. 145:17). His power, His knowledge, His wisdom, all mystify us.

But that which breaks the untilled soil of our hard hearts is none of the above. It is the righteousness of His love. It is the realization that the Sovereign of the universe stooped to become sovereign of our lives, that Infinity had regard for finitude. That is what breaks our hearts and causes us to say:

"That Thou canst think so well of me
And be the God Thou art
Is darkness to my intellect
But sunshine to my heart."

He does not need us.

He who reigns over myriads of worlds unsullied by sin—He need not claim this apostate planet, this one lost sheep, this foul ghetto of sin, this lone aberration that stains His handiwork.

But He does! He claims us as His own. We are His loyal subjects. By His mighty acts of love, Christ, the Lord of Creation, has become our sovereign of redemption.

We desperately need a Redeemer-Sovereign because we are all born sinners. "Behold, I was shapen in iniquity," the psalmist lamented, "and in sin did my mother conceive me" (Ps. 51:5). In Eden we were, by the sin of our first parents, conformed to the nature of Satan and made subjects of His earthly dominion. We are, in a spiritual sense, "dead on arrival." Dead to righteousness. Dead to obedience. Dead to the ways and will of God.

At birth we are victims of "inbred evil," prisoners of faulty genes, chained to perversities that we cultivate by constant use. We are driven slavishly from one demeaning habit—and its consequences—to another. Our appetite is fleshly. Our judgment is faulty. Our will is flabby. We don't know the will of God, we don't do the will of God, and worse, we don't even care!

In Satan's kingdom we suffer deception, delusion, and deceit. Satan's promises never come true. The consequences of serving him are never joyous. His priorities are never rational. He is a liar and a demagogue whose tyranny deludes and destroys.

But he is our original sovereign, and he rightly claims our allegiance.

Only the Redeemer-Sovereign can effect a change. Only by the miracle of the new birth, when we are recast from slaves of evil to subjects of righteousness, can our salvation be effected. Christ literally rescues us, in the words of Paul, from the "power of darkness" and translates "us into the kingdom of his dear Son" (Col. 1:13).

But the transition from death to life is not irreversible. The pages of history are filled with the sad examples of people who, having escaped from the evil kingdom, were subsequently deceived by genealogies and conjecturings, discouraged by trials and sufferings, and willingly went back to the sweet but poisonous leeks and onions of their former bondage (Num. 11:5).

Jesus warned, "No one who puts his hand to the plow and looks back is fit for service in the kingdom of God" (Luke 9:62, NIV). Peter, in graphic language, condemns those who, having begun in Christ, turn back as a "dog is turned to his own vomit again" (2 Peter 2:22).

Christ's reign in our hearts is conditional. Our conversion is conditional. We are inducted into our new relationship by a surrender that never is completed. Our initial experience is not enough, unless, like the thief on the cross, we die upon confession. If we live, we must persevere. Our love and trust must be sustained. We who were dead in sin at birth and who died to sin at conversion must throughout our lives "die daily."

The dethronement of Satan and the enthronement of Christ upon the seat of our souls is not an irrevocable trust. Christ reigns upon conditions spelled out in

His Word and exemplified in the life of every faithful subject. He demands complete and unequivocal obedience.

Christ's sovereignty requires of us total allegiance. He is a jealous God. Christ our sovereign does not permit us to have divided allegiance. The heart that expends any of love's energy upon former lusts or newfound perversities, or that withholds any of love's sacrifice in present service, is not worthy of His presence.

Our Redeemer-Sovereign can and will preserve us. His promise is that "no man is able to pluck [us] out of [His] Father's hand" (John 10:29).

But partial surrender won't work. "No one can serve two masters," Christ declared (Matt. 6:24). We don't have the luxury of a "no man's land" between each kingdom's borders, a demilitarized zone where neither Christ nor Satan rules. We cannot claim dual citizenship or diplomatic immunity.

Neither can we conceal some unspoken part of ourselves; to hide, like Achan, some private lust from the eyes of others is not to hide it from God. "Thou shalt love the Lord thy God with all thy heart, and with all thy soul, and with all thy mind," the Redeemer-Sovereign demands (Matt. 22:37). Our only acceptable response to that demand is "I surrender all, all to thee my blessed Saviour, I surrender all."

It is important that "this point be fully settled in every mind: If we accept Christ as a Redeemer, we must accept Him as a Ruler. We cannot have the assurance and perfect confiding trust in Christ as our Saviour until we acknowledge Him as our King and are obedient to His commandments" *(Faith and Works,* p. 16).

Christ's sovereignty requires of us total dependence. In God's kingdom there are rules—strict rules, just rules, righteous rules. Rules that are reflections of His character and very unlike those our flesh yearns to follow.

We do not have holy flesh; however, we may and must have holy wills. That is, totally committed desires. But until "mortals put on immortality" (1 Cor. 15:53), we will never live in holy flesh. And that means that our salvation is dependent upon a power higher than ourselves.

Yes, we grow, we progress, we move up the ladder of grace and obedience. We produce the fruits of righteousness—love, joy, long-suffering, goodness, mercy, faith. But not from anything innately good within us.

We do so because Christ captures and holds our wills. When through His Spirit He controls our lives, we walk no longer after the dictates of our flesh, but after the Spirit (Gal. 5:25). Because we abide in Him, we don't "continue to sin" (1 John 3:6, 9, NIV). Because we have been born of God, through faith we have "overcome the world" (1 John 5:4, NIV).

If this is our declaration, then, how do we explain our need of an advocate to mediate forgiveness continually before the Father? Why is Christ's advocacy necessary if we no longer sin?

Christ's advocacy is necessary because while the believers described in 1 John 3:6, 9 do err, they do not continue in sin. Though they sometimes fall, they do not "sin habitually." This is made clear in the statement: "While the followers of Christ have sinned, they have not given themselves to the control of evil" *(Testimonies,* vol. 5, p. 474).

We Christians do not plan, chart, design, and cherish our transgressions; nevertheless, we "all fall short of God's glorious ideal" (Rom. 3:23, TCNT). It is no wonder that Ellen White wrote: "We should remember that our own ways are not faultless. We make mistakes again and again. . . . No one is perfect but Jesus. Think of Him and be charmed away from yourself" *(That I May Know Him,* p. 136).

The fundamental fact of our condition is that even when we are not sinning (i.e., disobeying), we are still sinners. That is because in our flesh "dwelleth no good thing" (Rom. 7:18). What does dwell in the flesh? Only bad things: the fallenness of our birth, our perversity, our propensity to evil, which, though subdued by conversion, constantly strives for resuscitation and renewal of control.

John Calvin was right when, in describing the saint's dilemma, he observed: "Though sin ceases to reign, it continues to dwell in them in a perpetual cause of contention" *(Institutes,* p. 10).

Hence, our utter dependence upon Jesus—and in consequence, our happy discovery that, even though in this life we are never fully grown spiritually, in Jesus we are never ever forsaken. Christ does not abandon His place in our lives or cast us out each time we err. He judges our character "not by occasional good deeds or occasional misdeeds, but by the tendency of the habitual words and acts" *(Steps to Christ,* pp. 57, 58).

And then He gives us that most magnanimous of gifts: He places His own righteousness to our needy ledgers.

That is the meaning of the thought: "The only way in which he [the sinner] can attain to righteousness is through faith. By faith he can bring to God the merits of Christ, and the Lord places the obedience of His Son to the sinner's account. Christ's righteousness is accepted in place of man's failure" *(Selected Messages,* book 1, p. 367).

Christ is our merciful sovereign.

Our Sovereign demands our total effort. It is not true that His gift of merits obviates our trying. Melancthon summarized it well when he stated: "It is faith alone that saves; but the faith that saves is not alone."

We are not passive participants in the drama of redemption. We are not brought "stainless and blameless into the blaze of His presence" without effort on our part. To the contrary, Jesus mandates us to "violent" efforts in the salvation process (Matt. 11:12). We must, in Paul's words, "work out [our] own salvation with fear and trembling" (Phil. 2:12). We Christians must be militant, marching, warring, wrestling, running, fighting against the prince of darkness.

By our good works we frustrate Satan, denying his wishes; we please the Father, whose law we honor; we delight our Saviour, whose example we follow and by whom we are given pardon and forgiveness. But our fruits do not save us. Only the righteousness of Christ can do that. Our works make heaven happy, but they do not make heaven happen.

Someday when we move from "no condemnation" to "no separation," our struggle will be over. Then, having "fought the good fight" and "finished the race" (2 Tim. 4:7, NIV), having endured "to the end" (Matt. 24:13), we will hear the glad words "Well done, good and faithful servant" (Matt. 25:21), words that describe our endurance in the *kingdom of grace,* but not our fitness for the *kingdom of glory.*

That is accomplished solely by the blood of reconciliation and the life of sanctification given in our behalf by our merciful Servant/Sovereign.

Royalty is no longer in vogue in the nations of the world. The revolt of the people against despotism, begun at the French Revolution has all but eliminated monarchy as a system of governance in our day. The few examples of royalty that remain are for the most part ceremonial reflections of dynasties past.

In Europe and in other places of the world we see ornate edifices that display the lifestyles of yesterday's royalty. One of the more impressive is the Royal Monastery at El Escorial in Spain, just northeast of Madrid. There, in an exquisitely ornate and lavish rotunda named the Pantheon, lie the withered remains of many of Spain's kings and queens. Each of the 22 gold-trimmed coffins is mounted on four heavily bronzed lion's paws. In the center of each box, on a gilded plate with raised black lettering, is the name of the monarch whose remains it contains. The male rulers range from Charles V, holy Roman emperor (1500-1558), to King Alphonso XII (1857-1885); and the queens from Isabella I (1451-1504) to Isabella II (1830-1904).

It is all very impressive. One can almost hear trumpets and see strong, white steeds prancing along, bearing potentates who were undisputed rulers of all they surveyed—feared and revered by their subjects. But now in death they are merely cold statistics, curiosity pieces gazed upon by succeeding generations who can never fully understand what gave them such privilege and authority.

But not so with Jesus. Our righteous Sovereign is our ever-present, ever-living king.

Pilgrims mark His place of internment, but they need not gild His tomb. He is not there. Jesus died, but He did not remain dead. He in whom the Godhead dwelt bodily slept in death, but death did not sleep in Him. He rose and ascended on high—glorified and triumphant.

Our righteous Sovereign was denied recognition at birth and comfort at death. But when He returned to His throne He was engulfed by the echoing praises of adoring angels.

Now our Sovereign serves as our high priest, who "ever liveth to make intercession" for us (Heb. 7:25). His priestly ministry is necessitated by the fact that we shall have our sinful nature until we are provided with immortality. "The intercession of Christ in man's behalf in the sanctuary above is as essential to the plan of salvation as was His death upon the cross" *(The Great Controversy,* p. 489).

Soon the struggle on this earth will be ended. Soon He will declare, "He that is holy, let him be holy still" (Rev. 22:11). Soon He, in the words of hymn writer Isaac Watts, "shall reign where'er the sun does his successive journey's run; His kingdom stretch from shore to shore, Till moons shall wax and wane no more" *(Church Hymnary,* p. 317).

We, His grateful subjects, will then join the angels above and all of creation in eternal adoration. Our refrain will be: "Worthy is the Lamb that was slain to receive power, and riches, and wisdom, and strength, and honour, and glory, and blessing" (Rev. 5:12).

Christ is our righteous sovereign.

CHAPTER 6

CHRIST OUR RIGHTEOUS SEED

"Now to Abraham and his seed were the promises made. He saith not, And to seeds, as of many; but as of one, And to thy seed, which is Christ" (Gal. 3:16).

A seed is a kernel of life, the secret of by which each animate species perpetuates its order. Jesus is our righteous seed.

Christ is our righteous seed of humanity.

In Paul's impressive salutation to the Romans, he spoke these words about Christ: "Paul, a servant of Jesus Christ, called to be an apostle, separated unto the gospel of God, (Which he had promised afore by his prophets in the holy scriptures,) concerning his Son Jesus Christ our Lord, which was made of the seed of David according to the flesh" (Rom. 1:1-3).

Long years before Christ's birth, God said to Abraham: "And I will establish my covenant between me and thee and thy seed after thee in their generations for an everlasting covenant, to be a God unto thee, and to thy seed after thee. And I will give unto thee, and to thy seed after thee, the land wherein thou art a stranger, all the land of Canaan, for an everlasting possession; and I will be their God" (Gen. 17:7, 8).

Through the nation of Israel, the descendants of Abraham, the peoples of the earth were blessed. The Jews transmitted the laws of God through their teachings. They preserved the knowledge of the plan of salvation by the dramatizations of their sanctuary. But their most privileged contribution was that of being the physical progenitors of Christ, the promised Messiah.

Matthew, the careful chronicler of details, traced Christ's ancestry as "the son of David, the son of Abraham" (Matt. 1:1). After painstakingly listing 14 generations of Abraham's descendants, Matthew concluded: "And Jacob begat Joseph the husband of Mary, of whom was born Jesus, who is called Christ" (verse 16).

But the gospel writer makes it clear that Joseph's contribution was legal, not biological: "Now the birth of Jesus Christ was on this wise: When as his mother Mary was espoused to Joseph, before they came together, she was found with child of the Holy Ghost" (verse 18).

Luke quotes the angel's words: "The Holy Ghost shall come upon thee, and the power of the Highest shall overshadow thee: therefore also that holy thing which shall be born of thee shall be called the Son of God" (Luke 1:35).

The Spirit of God, who called forth all creation from an empty earth, provided the Incarnation from an empty womb. Christ came to us as a God/man, the miracle of Bethlehem. There will never be another like Him.

He could have come as a robust youth or a full-grown man ready to launch His career, but He appeared, as do all humans, as a helpless infant. By attaching to Mary's womb, Christ came into the world "our" way, identifying with our "nature." A virgin *conceived.* And that is how He came to be our righteous human seed.

Christ is our righteous seed of holiness.

Christ exceeds His ancestry in righteousness. David, at whom Nathan pointed the finger of chastisement; Jacob, whose strenuous wrestling was occasioned by the knowledge of His guilt; even Abraham himself, by whose lack of faith a son was sired whose descendants even now war angrily with his brother's children. These giants of history, these ancestors of flesh, were sinners.

But He was not.

Unlike His fathers, Christ was a perfect child and a holy man. He lived a flawless existence (1 Peter 2:22, 23). He prevailed without a nuance of disobedience—none of His earthly progenitors' weaknesses invaded His holy state. He came and He remained our righteous seed of holiness.

And we, "being born again, not of corruptible seed, but of incorruptible, by the word of God, which liveth and abideth forever" (1 Peter 1:23), are conformed into His image.

Christ's consequence in our lives is not simply sharpened intellects and social graces. His fruit is holiness. He who decreed the law of "cause and effect," who dictated that nature reproduce after its kind, functions that way in our hearts. His people are "trees of righteousness," and in them the Holy Seed produces the "fruit of holiness."

Paul testified to that when he said: "But now being made free from sin, and become servants to God, ye have your fruit unto holiness, and the end everlasting life" (Rom. 6:22). Isaiah explained: "As a teil tree, and as an oak, whose substance is in them, when they cast their leaves: so the holy seed shall be the substance thereof" (Isa. 6:13).

And of those declared believers in whom the Seed has not taken root, Jesus warned: "Now also the axe is laid unto the root of the trees: therefore every tree which bringeth not forth good fruit [fruits of righteousness] is hewn down, and cast into the fire" (Matt. 3:10).

But that is not His will for us. We are all elected, called, chosen to be His royal seed. We are invited to be part of the new Israel, His universal spiritual family.

A person is, after all, "not a Jew if he is only one outwardly," said Paul. "Nor is circumcision merely outward and physical. No, a man is a Jew if he is one inwardly; and circumcision is circumcision of the heart, by the Spirit, not by the written code. Such a man's praise is not from men, but from God" (Rom. 2:28, 29, NIV).

The miracle of holiness cannot be examined in terms of logic or human science. It is part and parcel of the mystery of godliness.

We cannot explain this reorientation of life, this transformation of thought, this redirecting of desires that the Holy Seed produces, but we have seen it work again and again. We know that it is real.

As the physical seed takes root in the earth and then bears fruit, so the spiritual seed germinates within our hearts, producing first the blade, then the leaf, then the stalk, then the branch, then the vine, and finally the fruit that holiness decrees.

Christ is our righteous seed of harvest.

In the Bible, the harvest, the time of reaping, the ingathering of crops, is symbolic of the end of the world. Our Lord spoke plainly about the final harvest. His command to His reaping angels will be to "gather ye together first the tares, and bind them in bundles to burn them: but gather the wheat into my barn" (Matt. 13:30).

His broken, bleeding body is the seed of life that makes the resurrection possible.

"I tell you the truth," Christ said, "unless a kernel of wheat falls to the ground and dies, it remains only a single seed. But if it dies, it produces many seeds" (John 12:24, NIV).

Christ is that kernel of wheat that fell to the ground. He is the seed that was sown in the furrow of the earth. He entered our world with "life, original, unborrowed, underived" *(Selected Messages,* book 1, p. 296); and He carried those qualities with Him into the grave. Christ, our seed of harvest, retained in His resting place all the powers He held when at Creation He "spake and it was done; . . . commanded, and it stood fast" (Ps. 33:9). The body wrapped in Joseph's new tomb contained no less prowess than had the Lord who clothed the worlds.

But had He remained in the ground, there could be no final harvest. "If Christ be not risen," Paul clarified, "then is our preaching vain, and your faith is also vain. . . . But now is Christ risen from the dead, and become the firstfruits of them that slept. For since by man came death, by man came also the resurrection of the dead" (1 Cor. 15:14-21).

We cannot fully comprehend the Incarnation or the Resurrection. These are on a higher plane than human reason can reach. But this much we do know. The tomb of our Holy Seed is empty; He has arisen!

Christ did not rise in response to His Father's call or the angel's trumpet voice. He rose at the sound of the internal time clock that He had set when He said, "Destroy this temple, and in three days I will raise it up" (John 2:19). "As Jonas was three days and three nights in the whale's belly; so shall the Son of man be three days and three nights in the heart of the earth" (Matt. 12:40).

Only by being the righteous seed of humanity could Christ qualify as our seed of harvest. That is because every seed bringeth forth its kind. A nonhuman seed must produce a nonhuman harvest. An unholy seed must bring forth an unholy harvest. Because Jesus is our holy human seed, He will bring forth a marvelous harvest, a holy nation of redeemed saints that "no man can number."

When will this resurrection, this harvest, be?

"When the fruit is brought forth," Christ said, "immediately he putteth in the sickle, because the harvest is come" (Mark 4:29). The state of the living church will determine the time of harvest.

"Christ is waiting with longing desire for the manifestation of Himself in His church. When the character of Christ shall be perfectly reproduced in His people, then He will come to claim them as His own" *(Christ's Object Lessons,* p. 69).

"Perfectly reproduced?" How can that be when our best hope is that incomplete state we call "relative perfection," and if, as John states, we lie when we say we have no sin (1 John 1:8)?

It seems so impossible. But it is possible. That this is not now our common experience results from our yielding to the world's competing values. That our lives, our characters, remain faulty is not a judgment on the Seed; it is a comment on the soil of our hearts. It is a reflection both upon our worldliness and Christ's great love in providing for us His robe to cover our struggling condition.

Christ our righteous seed established for us an example, a pattern for living, that is absolutely perfect: perfect in nature, perfect in motive, perfect in performance. "We cannot equal the pattern" *(Testimonies,* vol. 2, p. 549).

However, you and I can even now have "Christian perfection of the soul" *(Selected Messages,* book 2, p. 32). That is, we can have complete forgiveness of sins and the absolute surrender of will that Heaven requires. But until His coming we cannot be absolutely perfect in nature and performance. The enduring, though arrested and subdued, dynamics of our human state (unholy flesh) continues to soil our brightest deeds and render our highest obedience as "filthy rags" (Isa. 64:6).

When will Christ return? When will His people "perfectly reproduce" His character?

When those things are removed that "can be shaken . . . so that what cannot be shaken will remain" (Heb. 12:27, NIV). When the redeemed from among men will be "without fault before the throne of God" (Rev. 14:5). Only then will His sealed people perfectly reproduce the character of Christ.

That will be His signal to come. The harvest will be ready. The seed He has sowed will have done a complete work "after its kind" in the hearts of His trusting saints. But even then the reality of our unholy flesh—the fact that we are sinners even when we are not sinning—will necessitate His covering robe.

The words "Well done, thou good and faithful servant . . . enter" (Matt. 25:21) that the saved will hear will signify Christ's approval of our progress, but not His ratification of "our" righteousness.

Christ's righteous life, affirmed by the Resurrection, is our saving valedictory. His exit from the grave is proof positive of Heaven's acceptance of His ministry on our behalf. It is also a reminder of our need to accept His triumphs as our sufficient covering and His promise to return as our brightest hope.

Meanwhile, we cherish His prayer on our behalf: "I in them, and thou in me, that they may be made perfect in one" (John 17:23). We, His growing, trusting followers, know that this petition is being answered in our lives. We see the incontrovertible evidence of our union with Him in our growth in grace, even as we are covered by His righteousness, and we freely conclude:

> "Christ is the righteous bread we need,
> His is the righteous voice we heed,
> Christ is the righteous truth indeed;
> He is our righteous living seed.

Christ is our righteous seed.

WINDOWS ON HIS REPRESENTATION

CHAPTER 7

CHRIST OUR RIGHTEOUS SPOKESMAN

"Who is this that cometh from Edom, with dyed garments from Bozrah? this that is glorious in His apparel, travelling in the greatness of his strength? I that speak in righteousness, mighty to save" (Isa. 63:1).

A spokesman is one who speaks for another, a person whose credentials and credibility give needed influence in behalf of an individual or group whose situation requires it. Christ is our righteous spokesman.

Because of our desperate condition, we need someone to represent us in eternal matters. Jesus provides this representation in several critical ways.

Christ speaks through us.

We are His disciples, the sheep of His pasture, epistles of His grace sent forth to witness to His kingdom in a harsh, cruel world. Christ declared that our audience today would be a generation like the people of Sodom and Gomorrah and of Noah's time—intemperate, irreverent, insensitive to the Word of God (Luke 17:26, 27).

Paul said these people would be "lovers of their own selves, covetous, boasters, proud, blasphemers, disobedient to parents, unthankful, unholy, without natural affection, trucebreakers, false accusers, incontinent, fierce, despisers of those that are good, traitors, heady, highminded, lovers of pleasure more than lovers of God" (2 Tim. 3:1-4).

We are, as our Master warned, "sheep in the midst of wolves" (Matt. 10:16).

Christ gave us a distinguished but dangerous assignment. He told us we would be persecuted, delivered up, brought before kings and rulers, hated, even put to death, and that in all these ways we are His witnesses (Luke 21:12-16). For blundering, error-prone humans, this is a daunting task.

But Christ told us to disdain anxiety, promising, "[I will] give you a mouth and wisdom, which all your adversaries shall not be able to gainsay or resist" (verse 15). "It shall be given you in that same hour," He assured, "what ye shall speak" (Matt. 10:19).

How else could weak humans face the beings of evil who man the devil's kingdom with suicidal determination? How else can struggling Christians with so much self yet unconquered talk to those of like and less spiritual condition and see their lives changed? Before such odds we are all like Moses: ineloquent, slow of speech, and hesitant of tongue (Ex. 4:10).

But God's promise to Moses, His chosen spokesman—"Therefore go, and I will be with thy mouth, and teach thee what thou shalt say" (verse 12)—is no less sure, no less final, to us than to His servant then.

Aaron and his descendants became official channels of God's will throughout their generations. In private revelation and through the Urim and Thummim, God gave Israel His directions.

Now we who are a nation of priests (Rev. 1:6) speak today for Him. But it is not us who speak; it is Christ speaking through us, by His Spirit. We are effective transmitters of His grace only as He inspires our language and prospers our words.

Unless He speaks through us, no sinners will confess, no demons will flee, no storms will cease, no fevers will abate, no dry bones will live, no fruits of righteousness will blossom on the otherwise barren, lifeless stalks of humanity.

We have no healing virtue, no communicable good, no transmittable righteousness. Our only hope of productivity in His cause is His promise: "My grace is sufficient for thee: for my strength is made perfect in weakness" (2 Cor. 12:9).

Christ speaks to us.

When Christ was here on earth He spoke often of the Father's love for us. Brushing from the law the crusted debris of Pharisaical traditionalism, He revealed the Father as patient, caring, loving, just, honest, and fair. "He that hath seen me," He said, "hath seen the Father" (John 14:9).

We needed that. Satan had succeeded in making the Father appear to be an uncaring and arbitrary being, but Jesus explained the Father as a loving, long-suffering parent. He gave us a personal witness.

God the Father "at sundry times and in divers manners" (Heb. 1:1) spoke personally to the prophets in times past. From Eden to Bethlehem, He revealed Himself in many wondrous ways to the human race.

But Jesus, in whom "dwelleth all the fullness of the Godhead bodily" (Col. 2:9), gave us the ultimate view.

Today Christ still speaks to us. He does so in many ways: by experience, by nature, by prophecy, by circumstances. But He speaks most effectively to us by His blood, poured out at Calvary. His blood is, for every true believer, a "magnificent obsession," the "common denominator" of our spiritual thought; it attracts our attention, claims our allegiance, melts our hearts.

Christ's blood speaks eloquently of the Father's great heart, the Son's great love, the Spirit's great care. Above the cries of the demons of our flesh within us, above the never-ending cacophony of allurements outside us, the blood of Christ urges: "This is the way, walk ye in it" (Isa. 30:21); "Love not the world, neither the things that are in the world" (1 John 2:15); "Look unto me, and be ye saved, all the ends of the earth" (Isa. 45:22); and "If ye love me, keep my command-ments" (John 14:15).

Christ speaks in us.

Consider Paul's words to the Corinthian church: "And being absent now I write to them which heretofore have sinned, and to all other, that, if I come again, I will not spare: since ye seek a proof of Christ speaking in me, which to you-ward is not weak, but is mighty in you" (2 Cor. 13:2, 3).

Christ speaks in us by His Word, the Holy Scriptures. His Word *in us* pro-duces our conversion (1 Peter 1:23). His Word *in us* causes fruits of righteous-ness to grow (John 15:7, 8). His Word *in us* enables us to overcome (1 John 2:14). His Word *in us* provides us "staying power"; for, as the beloved apostle reminds us, when the Word of God remains in us, we shall "continue in the Son, and in the Father" (verse 24).

Paul, the great missionary-apostle, was always ready to encourage His hear-ers to embrace the Word. To the church in Corinth he wrote: "The testimony of Christ was confirmed in you" (1 Cor. 1:6). To the Galatian members he wrote: "I travail . . . until Christ be formed in you" (Gal. 4:19). To the Ephesian believers he wrote: "There is . . . one God and Father of all, who is above all, and through all, and in you all" (Eph. 4:4-6). To the Philippian Christians he wrote: "For it is God which worketh in you both to will and to do of his good pleasure" (Phil. 2:13).

He urged the Colossian believers to embrace "the riches of the glory of this mystery . . . which is Christ in you, the hope of glory" (Col. 1:27). And to "let the word of Christ dwell in you richly in all wisdom; teaching and admonishing one another in psalms and hymns and spiritual songs, singing with grace in your hearts to the Lord" (Col. 3:16).

To the faithful at Thessalonica Paul spoke of the "word of God, which effec-tually worketh also in you that believe" (1 Thess. 2:13). To Philemon he wished "that the communication of thy faith may become effectual by the acknowledg-ing of every good thing which is in you in Christ Jesus" (Philemon 6). And to the

Jewish converts he communicated his desire that God make them "perfect in every good work to do His will, working in you that which is well pleasing in His sight, through Jesus Christ; to whom be glory forever and ever" (Heb. 13:21).

Other New Testament authors also emphasized this truth.

Peter declared: "For if these things be in you, and abound, they make you that ye shall neither be barren nor unfruitful in the knowledge of our Lord Jesus Christ" (2 Peter 1:8). And the beloved John, in simple but glowing language, said: "Ye are of God, little children, and have overcome them: because greater is he that is in you, than he that is in the world" (1 John 4:4).

The natural result of the indwelling Christ is righteousness.

"If Christ be in you," Paul explained, "the body is dead because of sin; but the Spirit is life because of righteousness" (Rom. 8:10). This righteousness is certainly a gift to be sought for, prayed for, hoped for, worked for.

And in a sense, this righteousness wrought in us is also Christ's righteousness. This is why in our postconversion confession we declare: "I live; yet not I, but Christ liveth in me" (Gal. 2:20).

But the righteousness wrought by Christ's working in us differs from the righteousness that Christ bestows upon us. The former is the result of His power infused in us; the latter is the result of His covering bestowed upon us.

Christ speaks for us.

In addition to speaking through us and to us and in us, Christ must also speak *for us.* If His work *in us* were sufficient to qualify us for heaven, He would, having developed in us a perfect character, introduce us to the Father finished and full, without need of covering or further intercession.

But that is not the case. The Father's acceptance is not the result of what is worked in us; it is the consequence of what was worked for us.

Christ earned the right to be our spokesman. He earned it, first of all, by His incarnation. He became one of us. "In Christ we become more closely united to God than if we had never fallen. In taking our nature, the Saviour has bound Himself to humanity by a tie that is never to be broken" *(The Desire of Ages,* p. 25).

Christ knows our situation. He is a high priest who can be "touched with the feeling of our infirmities" (Heb. 4:15). He knows our earthly milieu, our global neighborhood. He ate our food and drank our water. He walked our streets. He breathed our air. He was here among us.

He became our hero, but He also became our brother and friend.

Now Christ is able to tell God all about us. A Child now of humanity, the Son of God is able to explain our condition, describe our hurts, relate the experience of being bound in human flesh, of living under the sentence of death, of being victims of a fate we did not seek and cannot escape.

He earned this right by His holiness.

While He was here He was absolute in surrender, singular in devotion, faultless in character. "For thirty years He lived the life of a perfect man, meeting the highest standard of perfection" *(Sons and Daughters of God,* p. 154). "His character was absolutely perfect, free from the slightest stain of sin" *(That I May Know Him,* p. 44). "Not for one moment was there in Him an evil propensity" *(SDA Bible Commentary,* Ellen G. White Comments, vol. 5, p. 1128).

He is able to speak effectively for us in heaven because He spoke no guile while on earth. His speech on earth reflected the purity of His soul, for "out of the abundance of the heart the mouth speaketh" (Matt. 12:34). Because the fountain of His soul was so absolutely pure, the words of His lips were faultlessly clean.

Simon Peter marveled that Christ, "when he was reviled, reviled not again; when he suffered, he threatened not; but committed himself to him that judgeth righteously" (2 Peter 2:23). In this way He earned the right to be "the mediator of the new covenant, and to the blood of sprinkling, that speaketh better things than that of Abel" (Heb. 12:24).

The blood is Christ's most effective word to us. That is certain. But it is also His most effective *voice for us.* Jesus' blood is what He holds up before the throne. His constant cry is "Father, My blood, My blood!"

And the blood of Christ works wonders. Because of the blood, the Father's justifiable wrath is abated, and sinners, unfinished in growth, bound still in unholy flesh, still very far from having "attained," are accepted.

Christ's petitioning on our behalf began before His return to the Father. In His great prayer of intercession shortly before His death (John 14-17), He pleaded for our unity (John 17:21-23), He pleaded for our joy (verse 13), He pleaded for our protection (verse 15), He pleaded for our sanctification (verses 17-19), and He pleaded for our eventual presence with Him (verse 24).

He also promised a "Comforter, which is the Holy Ghost, whom the Father will send in my name, he shall teach you all things, and bring all things to your remembrance, whatsoever I have said unto you" (John 14:26).

And then He died and ascended as our spokesman before the Father's throne.

Thus, with one hand Christ has grasped the feeble shoulders of humanity and with the other clasped the mighty hand of God. He has erected a bridge over sin's raging waters, a ladder to the heavens, a link to eternity. Christ is the Father's voice to us, and our voice to Him. He always hears us when we call—through Christ we have never-failing access to the Father.

"Who is this that cometh from Edom," the prophet Isaiah questioned, "with dyed garments from Bozrah?" (Isa. 63:1).

It is Christ, our righteous spokesman. He who travels in glorious apparel and greatness of strength, He who speaks in righteousness, mighty to save. Why is His apparel dyed? It is dyed because it was stained with His blood when He trod the winepress alone (verse 3). And why are His garments so bright? They are bright because they are righteous. And it is that righteousness that He shares with us.

This righteousness is absolutely essential because "only those who are clothed in the garments of His righteousness will be able to endure the glory of His presence when He shall appear with 'power and great glory'" *(Review and Herald,* July 9, 1908).

Christ no longer treads the winepress, and He is no longer alone. He is now acclaimed by myriads of adoring angels and unfallen beings of worlds above. However, His concern for our needs exceeds His love of their praise, and by His righteous intercession He pleads unceasingly for our otherwise hopeless condition.

Christ is our righteous spokesman.

CHAPTER 8

CHRIST OUR RIGHTEOUS SUBSTITUTE

"But if a messenger from heaven is there to intercede for him as a friend, to show him what is right, then God pities him and says, 'Set him free. Do not make him die, for I have found a substitute'" (Job 33:23, 24, TLB).

A substitute is a person who takes the place of someone else, one who is used or accepted in exchange, one who is utilized when the original is unavailable, unsuitable, or otherwise inadequate. Christ is our righteous substitute.

When he first fell, the first Adam disqualified himself for life in God's universe. Because of his sin, the God of Creation consigned his descendants to die, to return eventually to the nothingness from which they were created.

It didn't have to be. It was not heaven's intention.

God, unwilling to rule a universe of robots, gave the first Adam freedom of choice. Adam exercised that choice to sin.

But it was also free choice that effected our salvation. The second Adam exercised His choice to come to this earth and offer His life for our redemption. "When the fullness of time had come," wrote Paul, "God sent forth his Son, made of a woman, made under the law, to redeem them that were under the law, that we might receive the adoption of sons" (Gal. 4:4, 5).

The plan to send a second Adam, a substitute, was not formulated at the time of the first transgression. It was a provision "foreordained before the foundation of the world" (1 Peter 1:20).

The Substitute was to succeed where Adam had failed. He was to prove that Adam did not have to sin, that Adam could have prevailed over temptation, that the commandments are both possible to obey and profitable for the human race.

The Replacement for Adam, if He should succeed, would then become the new head of earth's occupants. The people of earth, held hostage in the diseased flesh wrought by the first Adam's disobedience, would, by the obedience of the Substitute, obtain redemption and thus regain right standing with God.

Not only would there be a second, successful Adam; there would be a new humanity. The inhabitants of earth would no longer be under heaven's condemnation.

God's justice could not prevent the natural consequences of sin. The descendants of Adam must die. But they are not left without hope!

The Father, whose mercy is as broad as His justice, agreed to allow the Son to substitute His absolute righteousness in the place of the failure of the first Adam and his struggling posterity. He pledged to accept not only His Son's life as our second Adam but also His dying as our second death, thus freeing us from the judicial consequences of sin.

But the success of the plan was not automatic. It depended, first of all, upon the ability of the Substitute to live in total compliance to the very laws that He Himself had established, laws that the fallen Lucifer had declared were impossible to keep. That supposed impossibility he loudly attested to by the tragedy of Eden.

And it would not be easy. The Substitute's obedience must be accomplished with the equipment of created beings, not those of the Creator. The second Adam had to prevail with capacities that in no way exceeded those of the first Adam.

And that is how Christ came.

It is true that He was all God, but He was also all human. Scripture describes Christ in dual personage as one "who, being in very nature God, did not consider equality with God something to be grasped, but made himself nothing, taking the very nature of a servant, being made in human likeness" (Phil. 2:6, 7).

"As man's substitute Christ [had to] conform to the law in every particular" (*The Desire of Ages,* p. 50). Thus, "Christ, at an infinite cost, by a painful process, mysterious to angels as well as to men, assumed humanity" (*SDA Bible Commentary,* Ellen G. White Comments, vol. 7, p. 915). And "like every child of Adam He accepted the results of the working of the great law of heredity" (*The Desire of Ages,* p. 49).

The physical, emotional, and rational energies with which Christ engaged the processes of His earthly life were those of the generation in which He was born. His was a generation worsened by 4,000 years of transgression. Clearly, the second Adam's nature was not superior to the first. His equipment was, in fact, weaker than that of the first Adam, with one exception: that of spiritual purity. He was born a holy child (Luke 1:35).

The first Adam before His fall had within "no corrupt principles . . . no corrupt propensities or tendencies to evil" and was "as faultless as the angels before God's throne" (*SDA Bible Commentary,* Ellen G. White Comments, vol. 1, p. 1083). The second Adam began in the same way. He took "His position at the head of humanity by taking the nature but not the sinfulness of man" *(ibid.,* vol. 7, p. 912).

And He stayed that way with handicaps that Adam did not have nor could have imagined. Every psychological and environmental advantage had been given to the first Adam.

But how different with our Substitute.

"Christ was tempted by Satan in a hundredfold severer manner than was Adam, and under circumstances in every way more trying" *(The Youth's Instructor,* June 2, 1898). He was assailed and opposed at every step of His life. "Satan contested every inch of ground, exerting his utmost power to overcome Him. Like a tempest, temptation after temptation beat upon Him" *(Signs of the Times,* Aug. 27, 1902).

But He did not sin.

Adam fell in a perfect Eden—Jesus succeeded in a wicked Nazareth. Bearing the burdens of His Father's honor and His people's redemption, Christ fought the battle of sin in our inadequate armor, these weak human bodies.

And He won! *The Lamb prevailed!*

The second Adam proved mightier than the first, the Substitute better than the original. By His sacrifice, the avenger has been stilled. He has become our new Head, our conquering Adam.

How thorough was His triumph? How complete?

It was total. Absolute.

Peter witnessed that He "did no sin, neither was guile found in his mouth" (1 Peter 2:22). John testified that "in him is no sin" (1 John 3:5). Paul confirmed: "For such an high priest became us, who is holy, harmless, undefiled, separate from sinners" (Heb. 7:26). And Jesus Himself summarized His spiritual triumph by saying: "The prince of this world cometh, and hath nothing in me" (John 14:30).

God needed that victory to vindicate His name, to exalt His justice, to magnify His law. We needed that victory to replace Adam's failure and gain a new origin. We needed it as a bank of righteousness rich enough and full enough to supply our salvation credits. Not to supplement our worthless goodness, but to replace it.

How vital is His obedience to our redemption?

Paul states that we were "reconciled to God by the death of his Son," but are "saved by his life" (Rom. 5:10). "Therefore as by the offence of one judgment came upon all men to condemnation; even so by the righteousness of one the free gift came upon all men unto justification of life. For as by one man's disobedience many were made sinners, so by the obedience of one shall many be made righteous" (verses 18, 19).

Ellen G. White gave us a very arresting explanation of this transaction: "We are accepted in the beloved. The sinner's defects are covered by the perfection and fullness of the Lord our righteousness. Those who with sincere will, with contrite heart, are putting forth humble efforts to live up to the requirements of God are looked upon by the Father with pitying, tender love; He regards such as obedient children, and the righteousness of Christ is imputed unto them" *(Our High Calling,* p. 51).

Consider also the following statements: "Having made us righteous through the imputed righteousness of Christ, God pronounces us just, and treats us as just. He looks upon us as His dear children" *(Selected Messages,* book 1, p. 394). "The Father beholds not your faulty character, but He sees you as clothed in My perfection" *(The Desire of Ages,* p. 357). "In order to meet the requirements of the law, our faith must grasp the righteousness of Christ, accepting it as our righteousness" *(Review and Herald,* Nov. 1, 1892). "Righteousness without a blemish can be obtained only through the imputed righteousness of Christ" *(ibid.,* Sept. 3, 1901).

And in excellent summation: "The only way in which [the sinner] can attain to righteousness is through faith. By faith he can bring to God the merits of Christ, and the Lord places the obedience of His Son to the sinner's account. Christ's righteousness is accepted in place of man's failure" *(Selected Messages,* book 1, p. 367).

Does this mean that the provisions the Substitute has made on our behalf weaken or cancel our obligation to good works and personal Christian endeavor? Does our faith in the marvelous victory of the second Adam and our newly gained status as heirs in the family of God negate our concern for individual striving?

Paul answers unequivocally no.

"Work out your own salvation with fear and trembling," the apostle admonished the young church (Phil. 2:12). James declared: "Faith, if it hath not works, is dead" (James 2:17). Christ Himself commanded His followers to "strive to enter in at the strait gate: for many, I say unto you, will seek to enter in, and shall not be able" (Luke 13:24).

But, then, are the consequences of our strivings redemptive? Can we by our good works satisfy the high and holy requirements of the law, thus allowing us to succeed where Adam failed?

No! Our strivings quantify us, but they do not qualify us. Our overcoming efforts develop within us the "excellence of grace," but they do not provide us with entrance into glory. The sinful bodies in which we reside are perpetual barriers to life in the presence of Him whose absolute purity makes Him a consuming fire.

The good fruits that our lives exhibit are spotted with the diseases of the vessel in which they are housed. Our spiritual progress is never complete. Our present state remains unfinished. That is why our truest praise is that which states:

"By His perfect obedience He has satisfied the claims of the law, and my only hope is found in looking to Him as my substitute and surety, who obeyed the law perfectly for me" *(Selected Messages,* book 1, p. 396).

The need of the righteousness of Christ by even the "born again" Christian is demonstrated further in the following statements: "The closer you come to Jesus, the more faulty you will appear in your own eyes; for your vision will be clearer, and your imperfections will be seen in broad and distinct contrast to His perfect nature" *(Steps to Christ,* pp. 64, 65).

"When we are clothed with the righteousness of Christ, we shall have no relish for sin; for Christ will be working with us. We may make mistakes, but we will hate the sin that caused the suffering of the Son of God" *(Messages to Young People,* p. 338).

"When it is in the heart to obey God, when efforts are put forth to this end, Jesus accepts this disposition and effort as man's best service, and He makes up for the deficiency with His own divine merit" *(Selected Messages,* book 1, p. 382).

The description of us as striving but faulty children of God is apt. We do have imperfections and deficiencies, and we do make mistakes. That is the urgency of Paul's desire to "be found in him, not having mine own righteousness, which is of the law, but that which is through the faith of Christ, the righteousness which is of God by faith" (Phil. 3:9).

This makes it possible to say emphatically that the *gift* of righteousness is superior to the *works* of righteousness. Our works are conditional; His gift is final. Our works are partial; His gift is complete. Our works are encouraging; His gift is ennobling. Our works are comparative; His gift is superlative.

Christ is our incomparable kinsman, our second Adam, our saving substitute. We do not have adequate terms with which to praise Him for His wonderful acts.

But the day is approaching when the two Adams will meet again. The Adam of Eden, raised and redeemed, will stand before the Adam of Gethsemane, exalted and esteemed. We shall thank Him then. With repeated refrains of praise we will cast our crowns at His pierced feet.

Then, relieved of the curse of sin, freed from the inbred weaknesses that now defile our best endeavors, we will praise Him appropriately for having had pity upon our poor estate, for stepping into the breach, for condescending to do for us what no other being could accomplish.

Until then, let us offer as appropriate praise these words of encouragement: "Thank God that we are not dealing with impossibilities. We may claim sanctification. We may enjoy the favor of God. We are not to be anxious about what Christ and God think of us, but about what God thinks of Christ, our Substitute" *(Selected Messages,* book 2, pp. 32, 33).

Christ is our righteous substitute.

CHAPTER 9

CHRIST OUR RIGHTEOUS SERVANT

"And whosoever will be chief among you, let him be your servant: even as the Son of man came not to be ministered unto, but to minister, and to give his life a ransom for many" (Matt. 20:27, 28).

A servant is a person who is subordinated to others. He or she is designated to provide for the needs and comforts of more fortunate persons. A servant toils at menial tasks for minimal pay. Christ is our righteous servant.

Christ is our servant in the status that He assumed.

Our Saviour came unheralded, unrecognized, unhonored. He was born in a cattle stall of peasant parents, in the poorest of neighborhoods. He was reared "on the wrong side of the tracks," in Nazareth, a city known for its perversity. Christ was, in Isaiah's imagery, "a root out of a dry ground" (Isa. 53:2).

When Christ reached manhood, His status did not improve. A poor, itinerant Preacher, He had no investment capital, no interest-bearing accounts—not even a home or place to claim as His own.

He was always borrowing things. He borrowed a boat from which to teach the people. He borrowed some fish and loaves with which to feed them. He borrowed a coin with which to demonstrate God's claim versus Caesar's. He borrowed a room in which to eat the "last supper" and a donkey on which to ride to that final meal. His friends had to solicit a tomb in which to lay his lacerated body.

His own personal assessment of His net worth was thus: "Foxes have holes, and the birds of the air have nests; but the Son of Man hath not where to lay his head" (Matt. 8:20).

He was God in disguise. The Creator in earthly apparel. The King in servant's likeness.

At times the glory of His eternal self penetrated His human exterior. When He rebuked Satan in the wilderness (Matt. 4:10). When He expelled traffickers from the Temple (Matt. 21:12, 13). At His response to the mob, "I am he" (John

18:6). When He told the priests at His trial, "Hereafter shall ye see the Son of man sitting on the right hand of power, and coming in the clouds of heaven" (Matt. 26:64). When answering Pontius Pilate's query "Art thou the King of the Jews?" He responded, "Thou sayest" (Matt. 27:11). At such times, wrote Ellen G. White, "divinity flashed through humanity" *(The Youth's Instructor,* Nov. 21, 1895). His human exterior proved too frail to contain the God who dwelt within.

But those partial revelations were few and fleeting. Christ's modus operandi was that of a man, not a God.

The prophet Isaiah foresaw Him and said He would have "no form nor comeliness; . . . there is no beauty that we should desire him" (Isa. 53:2).

The human form taken by the Son of God was not particularly attractive, certainly not nearly so as artists wish Him on canvas. "His height was a little above the general size of man" *(Spiritual Gifts,* p. 119). But so ordinary was His appearance that John, who searched for Him daily, did not know Him when He appeared. And Nathanael, seeing Him, wondered, "Could this man, who bore the marks of toil and poverty, be the Messiah?" *(The Desire of Ages,* p. 139).

Christ's disciples came to know His true identity, but the multitude never understood. They could not see that the poor Babe who cooed in the manger was the Being who "spake, and it was done; [who] commanded, and it stood fast" (Ps. 33:9). They could not see that He who plucked the corn was the "I AM" who made the soil, that the Prophet who stilled the storm was the Prince who created the heavens, that the dying Man who hung upon the cross was the Majesty who had strung out the stars.

The spirit of Christ contrasts sharply with that of Lucifer. Lucifer, now Satan, aspired to be like God; Jesus, who is God, agreed to be like us. Lucifer sought position in the councils of divinity; Jesus accepted participation in the misery of humanity.

Christ was Son of God and Son of man, Michael and archangel, Immanuel—God with us—Lord of the universe but servant to sinners. The King voluntarily became a pauper. The righteous Judge accepted punishment of death for the guilty criminal! "Who," the prophet Isaiah asked, "hath believed our report?" (Isa. 53:1). It is amazing, staggering, mysterious, awesomely wonderful—but true! God became our righteous servant.

Christ is our servant in the ministry He performed.

In characterizing His own service, Jesus stated: "The Son of man came not to be ministered unto, but to minister" (Mark 10:45). Expanding upon this self-summary of His labors, Christ adopted the job description prepared by Isaiah centuries before:

"The Spirit of the Lord is on me, because he has anointed me to preach good news to the poor. He has sent me to proclaim freedom for the prisoners and recovery of sight for the blind, to release the oppressed, to proclaim the year of the Lord's favor" (Luke 4:18, NIV).

John, commenting upon the volume of good accomplished in Christ's short ministry on earth, concluded: "And there are also many other things which Jesus did, the which, if they should be written every one, I suppose that even the whole world itself could not contain the books that should be written" (John 21:25).

The good that Christ accomplished is all the more wondrous when we remember the condition of society at the time of His appearance.

Isaiah prophesied that at Christ's first coming "the darkness shall cover the earth, and gross darkness the people" (Isa. 60:2). Darkness is an ample metaphor for the spiritual, mental, and physical debauchery to which mankind had fallen by the time of Jesus' birth. Four thousand years of decline had rendered Adam and Eve's posterity a diseased, demented, debilitated conglomerate of limited longevity.

By the time of Christ's birth, humanity had reached its lowest ebb. It had not been easy. That it had taken Satan 4,000 years to drag us to the brink of self-annihilation is a tribute to the God in whose image we were made. But finally, the fall that began with the disobedience in Eden culminated with the rejection at Bethlehem.

Angels sang at Christ's birth, but there was little for people who lived at that time to sing about. Minds were almost completely given over to superstition, intemperance, and idolatry. Bodies were easy prey for epidemics that swept over towns and villages like tidal waves, crippling and destroying whole families of helpless sufferers. Infant mortality was high, and large numbers of children were born disfigured, with no hope of prostheses or other corrective assistance.

Leprosy was rampant. Blindness was epidemic. Mental illness was common-place. People everywhere were afflicted by numbing unrelieved pain—without the help of immunizations, inoculation, or anesthesia.

With the science of healing still largely undiscovered, physicians pricked sores and made crude incisions with the jagged edges of contaminated instruments. The cures were often worse than the diseases. People lived out their brief days in darkness and suffering, without hope or help.

Then Jesus came!

"The light," stated John, shone forth "in the darkness." The most glorious years of earth's history were about to ensue. The Great Physician was among us!

The Fountain of Life was here! Sickness and pain could not abide His presence. All who came to Him in honest search of relief were healed.

The lame, the lepers, the deaf, the blind, all left glorifying the Son of God for His healing power. Villages through which He passed were left with a zero hospital census. Those merely touched by His shadow were healed. Even the dead revived when He spoke. Physicians, apothecaries, and morticians were temporarily put out of business when Christ was near.

But a toll was exacted from our righteous Servant. Jesus worked among us with human vitality. He worked the works of His Father, but it was an earthen vessel that housed the treasure. He pursued His mission with the endurance of a man, not the stamina of God.

He was greatly pained by His long hours of ceaseless labor: "Not until the last sufferer had been relieved did Jesus cease His work. . . . He often dismissed His disciples to visit their homes and rest; but He gently resisted their efforts to draw Him away from His labors. All day He toiled, teaching the ignorant, healing the sick, giving sight to the blind, feeding the multitude" *(The Desire of Ages,* p. 259).

Christ is our servant in His continuing ministry in heaven.

"But this man," Paul wrote, "because he continueth ever, hath an unchangeable priesthood. Wherefore he is able also to save them to the uttermost that come unto God by him, seeing he ever liveth to make intercession for them" (Heb. 7:24, 25).

Many similarities may be seen between the services of the priests who lived in Bible days and the ministry of Christ, our heavenly high priest. There are some dissimilarities as well. One is the necessity of succession because of disability or death. In the above scripture Paul is reminding us that, unlike earthly priests, Christ, our righteous servant lives forever. His is an unchangeable priesthood.

When Christ came into the world, the Godhead integrated humanity; when He returned to heaven, humanity integrated the Godhead. He returned forever "to retain His [human] nature in the heavenly courts, an everlasting pledge of the faithfulness of God" *(Selected Messages,* book 1, p. 258).

Some people change when their fortunes are reversed for the better; they act differently "when their ship comes in." A new degree. A new job with higher income. These have blurred the memory of many as to who they really are and where they took root. Some who have climbed the totem pole of success don't want their new colleagues to see them with their old friends, especially the humble folk back home. They change. They deny their background.

But not Jesus. Our righteous Servant is "the same yesterday, and to day, and for ever" (Heb. 13:8). He not only remembers us; He serves us continually in vital ministry before His Father.

The primary element of His service for us is the application of His blood. The priests of antiquity killed the sacrifice and sprinkled its blood before the ark with prayers of forgiveness for themselves and the people. Jesus, our righteous servant, both priest and victim, both offering and offerer, pleads not for Himself—He knew no sin—but for us.

And we need His blood not only to cover our past, but to provide forgiveness for our present mistakes as well. That is why John wrote: "Little children, these things write I unto you, that ye sin not. And if any man sin, we have an advocate with the Father, Jesus Christ the righteous" (1 John 2:1).

Forgiveness for what? For envy, for jealousy, for suspicion, for coldness to others, for criticism, for gossiping, for laziness, for wasting time, for anger, for neglecting duties, for ingratitude, for wicked imaginations, for wandering thoughts on the holy Sabbath day, for unholy desires. Even as we are being sanctified, we are still being justified. We are continually in need of forgiveness.

And that brings us to the second element of His present servanthood: the offering to us of His robe of righteousness.

You and I are not finished yet. That is why Christ's robe is still necessary. We may have been transformed in heart, yes. But we still reside in defective human bodies. We retain our unholy flesh. To say that we have unholy flesh is to own that there is something fundamentally evil at our spiritual core, to confess that even though our wills or desires are completely surrendered, our basic urges remain defective.

This fact is the reason for our desperate need of our righteous Servant's present help. The following statement portrays it well: "The religious services, the prayers, the praise, the penitent confession of sin ascend from true believers as incense to the heavenly sanctuary, but passing through the corrupt channels of humanity, they are so defiled that unless purified by blood, they can never be of value with God. They ascend not in spotless purity, and unless the Intercessor [Servant] who is at God's right hand presents and purifies all by His righteousness, it is not acceptable to God" (*Selected Messages,* book 1, p. 344).

Christ, who knelt before His disciples with the water and the towel, instituting the ordinance of humility and cleansing, now stands before the Father with His blood and His robe, effecting for us forgiveness and sanctification. Because the robe has no crooked seams, no smudges, no lint, no stain or faulty construction; because it is spotless and clean, the Father accepts it in the place of our sinful flesh, and we are thus fitted for heaven.

Our good works are indications. But only Christ's blood is corrective, and only His robe is redemptive. It is to Him that we must appeal.

Christ is our righteous servant.

WINDOWS ON
HIS INITIATIVE

CHAPTER 10

CHRIST OUR RIGHTEOUS SABBATH

"There remaineth therefore a rest to the people of God. For he that is entered into his rest, he also hath ceased from his own works, as God did from his. Let us labour therefore to enter into that rest, lest any man fall after the same example of unbelief" (Heb. 4:9-11).

The Sabbath is a rest, a respite and relief from labor, a refreshing of the mind and body that fosters renewal through focused communion with God. Christ is our righteous Sabbath.

There are many man-made substitute sabbaths, attractive but deceptive theories that propose relief and revitalization yet fail to provide spiritual renewal.

Their names are legion: Communism, secularism, capitalism, humanism, socialism, individualism, existentialism, etc. All offer harbors to which our tired, beleaguered, suffering citizenry can turn for rest and assurance.

But these are unable to fulfill their promises.

We desperately need rest. We need rest from armed conflict and terrorism. We need rest from oppression, from deception, from greed, from the many social ills that engulf us. More fundamentally, we need rest from sin—the sickness that spawns all other dysfunctions. That rest is found only in Christ, our righteous Sabbath.

Most philosophical and political constructs contain elements of good. The idolatrous Babylonians gave us quality architecture. The Greeks, who glorified myth, built a system of philosophy that shaped Western thought for centuries. The Romans, though immersed in Caesar worship, provided a legal system that forms the basis for present-day jurisprudence.

In fact, Paul reminded us that even the heathen, "who do not have the law," sometimes "do by nature things required by the law" (Rom. 2:14, NIV).

The philosophical systems of the Greeks and Romans were not intentionally evil. But mixed with their many helpful suggestions of right were contrary principles of wrong.

Eugene A. Nida highlights the issue when he commented: "The struggle between Greco-Roman religion and Christianity was on the point of exclusivism. The Greek world would gladly have put a statue of Jesus Christ in the Parthenon at Rome and exalted Him as another great religious thinker" *(Customs and Cultures,* p. 42).

But Christian obedience does not countenance divided loyalties, diluted truth, or shared allegiance. Christ is, for us, not simply "another"; He is *the* only, blessed, hallowed, sanctified Son of God. Just as no other day can convey those blessings we need except the day Christ sanctified, no other Saviour can effect peace between us and heaven. He is our righteous Sabbath.

The practical lessons of Sabbathkeeping clearly amplify the benefits of life with Christ. And one such lesson is *obedience.*

We are expected to *prepare* for the Sabbath, God's holy day of rest; in fact, the day before the Sabbath, Friday, is referred to in the Bible as "the preparation" (Matt. 27:62; Mark 15:42). Proper preparation would include waxed floors, clean tiles, washed cars, empty sinks, vacuumed rugs, polished shoes—whatever we can do to anticipate fellowship with the God of the Sabbath.

This physical purity that true Sabbathkeeping fosters is a symbol of the spiritual purity, the overcoming of sin, that accompanies rest in Jesus. "Entering into His rest" requires preparation of heart—holiness. It demands confession of transgressions and strict obedience to His will. Proper preparation for the Sabbath mirrors the process whereby He who pronounced "It is good" to His week of creative work pronounces "Well done" to our daily labors.

Another lesson of Sabbathkeeping is *trust.*

While the Sabbath stands as an enduring reminder of our obedience *to* Christ, an even more forceful instruction it provides is our dependence *upon* Christ. This lesson of trust was driven home daily during Israel's 44-year miracle of the manna (Ex. 16). No manna fell on the seventh day, and that which fell on the sixth was the only kind that did not spoil.

Sabbathkeeping is an act of dependence no less demanding for us than for our ancient counterparts. We trust that our rest from labor will not spoil our economic situation, that it will not bring disadvantage upon our business, that it will not lower our level of sustenance.

Sabbathkeepers are sometimes forced to change jobs or occupations, to alter appointments, to reschedule examinations, to reshuffle itineraries. On that day they absent themselves from all business and social affairs. But they do so in confident assurance that the Lord of the universe, whose moral law they obey, will protect and provide for them.

The legitimate labor of the six days that precede the Sabbath has no place on those sacred hours. These activities are not sinful, but neither are they consistent with Sabbath principles. Our works of charity are not in vain. They are pleasing to God, profitable, proper. For them we will, as we are taught in the parable of the faithful steward (Luke 19), be rewarded. However, these deeds are not holy; they do not save us. The Sabbath rest confirms that our act of trust, not our trust in acts, is our most vital posture.

To enter into rest with Christ is to acknowledge that His verdict "It is good" upon our everyday accomplishments is not His final commendation. That approval is provided by our trust in His perfect life, which covers us.

In order for us to enter into His rest, we must admit that our best is not good enough, that salvation is the consequence of His work—not ours.

As the Sabbath was fashioned to satisfy our human needs (Mark 2:27), so Christ's righteousness was given to cover our human inadequacies (Rom. 5:17-19). The former is a symbol of heavenly regard; the latter is a consequence of divine sacrifice, the acceptance of which is our highest obedience.

Those who enter into His rest must confess that Christ does for us what we cannot do for ourselves; that before the judgment bar we must all "stand still, and see the salvation of the Lord" (Ex. 14:13); that our Sabbath Lord, by a process to which we make no contribution, is preparing a place for us.

That is the essence of the counsel that "no one take the limited, narrow position that any of the works of man can help in the least possible way to liquidate the debt of his transgression. This is a fatal deception. . . . All that man can possibly do toward his own salvation is to accept the invitation, 'Whosoever will, let him take the water of life freely'" (*SDA Bible Commentary,* Ellen G. White Comments, vol. 6, p. 1071).

Yet another lesson of Sabbathkeeping is *belief.*

Canaan was promised to Israel as its happy rest. Four hundred years of slavery was to have been followed by a triumphant existence in a land of milk and honey.

Their failure to enter this rest was described in the apostle Paul's lament: "Who were they who heard and rebelled? Were they not all those Moses led out of Egypt? And with whom was he angry for forty years? Was it not with those who sinned, whose bodies fell in the desert? And to whom did God swear that they would never enter his rest if not to those who disobeyed? So we see that they were not able to enter, because of their unbelief" (Heb. 3:16-19, NIV).

Unbelief has always been a precursor to pain and loss. Unbelief caused Cain to offer a bloodless sacrifice, Lot's wife to turn back toward Sodom, Uzzah to reach for the falling ark, Jacob to scheme for the birthright, Moses to smite the rock, the Israelites to make a golden calf, Abraham to father Ishmael, the Jews, in their unbelief, to crucify their Messiah, thus nullifying their position as the chosen nation.

And how is it with us, modern Israel? Are we better than they? We are not! Our destructive unbelief is the cause of our lengthened pilgrimage.

That lack of belief is lived at polar extremes. It is lived, on the one hand, by those who refuse to believe that "a holy temper, a Christlike life, is accessible to every repenting, believing child of God." And that "as the Son of man was perfect in His life, so His followers are to be perfect in their life" *(The Desire of Ages,* p. 311).

But it is also seen in the contrary class: those who cannot accept the grand but simple truth that "Christ looks at the spirit, and when He sees us carrying our burden with faith, His perfect holiness atones for our shortcomings. When we do our best, He becomes our righteousness" *(Selected Messages,* book 1, p. 368).

But even if the Israelite nation had entered Canaan immediately, their trials would not have been eliminated. Canaan, the land of promise, had to be conquered, its land cultivated, its wilderness tamed, its inhabitants subdued.

Such is our need and our experience. Entering into fellowship with Christ extricates us from the former domination of sin. Conversion frees us from the kingdom of darkness.

But we soon discover that in the kingdom of grace there is still much land to conquer, much self to subdue, and that dwelling in Canaan is a life of "bound freedom"—that is, we are *bound* by our sinful nature, but *freed* by His sinless life. To those who will not believe this simple but marvelous truth, Christ is not a place of rest, a rock of refuge, but a "stone of stumbling."

Among the more memorable experiences of travel is viewing statues and monuments erected in countries and cities to commemorate local heroes and events. Often placed upon massive columns, these structures display champions of reformation and revolution, people whose acts of courage brought liberation to suffering masses.

One of the best-known statues in the world, however, does not represent a particular individual, but an idea. Towering and noble, it stands at the head of the Hudson River, welcoming, as it has for centuries, immigrants from all over the world. This "grand old lady" lifts her torch high above the harbor, boldly proclaiming: "Give me your tired, your poor, your huddled masses yearning to breathe free."

That invitation is not unlike the invitation that Jesus extends to us. He calls us to liberty in Him. The sad fact, however, is that America—burdened with its burgeoning rates of crime, divorce, and suicide; disgraced with its searing epidemics of drug addiction and venereal disease—today belies the claims of its harbor guardian.

Instead of the utopia our founders planned, we have become a stronghold of immorality, a cauldron of vice and hatred. In this land so grandly marked by freedom's torch, children are abused, minorities oppressed, women demeaned. Homeless people shiver in cardboard boxes on wintry nights, and an army of mentally ill roam our streets in uncontrolled misery. Our cities have rotted. Our morals have receded. The promise has not materialized.

But it is not so with those who seek refuge in Christ.

Burdened and heavy ladened, they come to Him and discover instant relief and eternal joy. Hungry for peace, yearning to be free from sin's oppression, they come and discover that in His "presence is fulness of joy," that at His "right hand there are pleasures evermore" (Ps. 16:11).

They come and find security in His love, guidance in His law, forgiveness in His blood, comfort in His grace, and covering under His robe. That is why the jubilant Paul could write of his unearned, undeserved acceptance with the Father as being "found in him, not having mine own righteousness, which is of the law, but that which is through the faith of Christ" (Phil. 3:9).

That is a provision too great to ignore, an offer too grand to refuse. "Let us labour therefore to enter into that rest" (Heb. 4:11).

Christ is our righteous Sabbath.

CHAPTER II

CHRIST OUR RIGHTEOUS SUN OF HEALING

"But unto you that fear my name shall the Sun of righteousness arise with healing in his wings; and ye shall go forth, and grow up as calves of the stall" (Mal. 4:2).

The sun is that luminous orb around which the earth and the other planets of our solar system revolve. Although it is 93 million miles away, the sun is the source of all the earth's radiant energy. The sun is absolutely essential to all aspects of our being. Christ is our righteous sun of healing.

Christ is the "light" of our universe. When He is visible, it is morning and our hearts are bright and warm and happy. When in the course of events we lose view of Him, it is night, dark, cold, and foreboding. Christ is "the true light," the beloved apostle testified, "that gives light to every man" (John 1:9, NIV).

The kingly sun, in never-failing beneficence, beams its blessings continually upon our planet; and so does our Lord, the Sun of righteousness, radiate continuously life-giving power. John's words are true: "All things were made by him; and without him was not any thing made that was made. In him was life; and the life was the light of men" (verses 3, 4).

But the orb that gladdens our world is also capable of awesome destruction. Its rays can blister and sear, blast and burn. But screened by the regulating gases of the atmosphere, the sun beams energy that inhibits the growth of harmful bacteria and conveys life-giving powers to our earth.

Jesus is a cleansing power. He came to heal and to restore. He came to rebuke the physical and spiritual diseases of suffering mankind.

Isaiah, struck by the moral paucity of suffering humanity, said of our moral condition: "The whole head is sick, and the whole heart faint. From the sole of the foot even unto the head there is no soundness in it; but wounds, and bruises, and putrifying sores: they have not been closed, neither bound up, neither mollified with ointment" (Isa. 1:5, 6).

Jeremiah, pleading for relief of our spiritual dilemma, asked: "Is there no balm in Gilead; is there no physician there?" (Jer. 8:22). The he answered eloquently for God: "They that spoil thee shall be a spoil, and all that prey upon thee will I give for a prey. For I will restore health unto thee, and I will heal thee of thy wounds, saith the Lord" (Jer. 30:16, 17).

The Father pitied us. But pity was not enough. God needed someone to redeem this lost creation, someone to heal our maladies and eradicate our sicknesses.

Jesus is that someone. Through that Instrument God sent truth and righteousness and forgiveness and healing. By Him we receive both the knowledge of a better possibility and the power to receive it. He is our sun of healing.

In days past, doctors were general practitioners, treating any and all the infirmities of the body. Today most physicians are specialists, maximizing their skills and knowledge in focused fields. In fact, there are few generalists left in any of today's professions. We seem to have become, for the most part, a society of scholars and workers learning "more and more about less and less."

But Jesus is a specialist in all of our sicknesses. There is nothing that afflicts us that He cannot cure, no strain of transgression that He cannot heal. In His hands we find love for our anger, faith for our doubts, courage for our fears, peace for our passion, hope for our despair, solace for our disappointments, and forgiveness for our guilt. He "healeth all thy diseases," the psalmist wrote (Ps. 103:3).

Christ heals our hurts.

Christ said: "He [the Father] hath sent me to heal the brokenhearted" (Luke 4:18). And He does.

Mothers who wash blood from the marble slabs where lay the mangled bodies of their children know. Children who visit graves of parents removed by accident and disease know. Widowed spouses who sit alone in homes once bright with love but darkened now by death know. Christ heals our hurts, our broken spirits.

Our burdens sometimes overwhelm us. Suffering the blight of unexpected tragedy and unavoidable disappointment, we sometimes are trapped in the prison of depression, condemned, it seems, to a meaningless, unhappy existence.

But Jesus, the psalmist says, is a "very present help in trouble" (Ps. 46:1). In the words of the hymn, Christ is a "mighty Rock in a weary land . . . a shelter in the time of storm" *(SDA Hymnal,* No. 528). He is a table in the wilderness. Even when we "walk through the valley of the shadow of death" (Ps. 23:4), He is a comforting presence.

When floods overflow us and fires of trial oppress us, we feel His loving touch, we hear His voice of comfort. We are energized by His presence, resuscitated by His love, healed by the Sun of righteousness who shines upon our hearts in the penetrating promises of His holy Word.

Sometimes the Sun of healing is obscured by the mist of trouble. But we have learned that behind the clouds the sun is still shining. And that "heaven and earth are no wider apart today than when shepherds listened to the angels' song. Humanity is still as much the object of heaven's solicitude as when common men of common occupations met angels at noonday, and talked with the heavenly messengers in the vineyards and the fields. To us in the common walks of life, heaven may be very near" *(The Desire of Ages,* p. 48).

Christ heals us of our oppression.

"God anointed Jesus of Nazareth with the Holy Ghost and with power: who went about doing good, and healing all that were oppressed" (Acts 10:38).

We are born with our burdensome yokes: idiosyncracies, manias, phobias, our various predispositions to err. And we inevitably add to our inherited woes the cultivated evils that drag us down. It all comes from Satan. His arsenal contains the diseases that oppress our bodies, the guilt that oppresses our consciences, the misfortune that oppresses our spirits. These are all His tools to derange and destroy.

But Satan's tools are reducible, even eradicable, by Christ, our sun of healing.

His pledge to heal our oppression is nowhere more powerfully expressed than in His comforting assurance: "Blessed be ye poor: for your's is the kingdom of God. Blessed are ye that hunger now: for ye shall be filled. Blessed are ye that weep now: for ye shall laugh. Blessed are ye, when men shall hate you, and when they shall separate you from their company, and shall reproach you,and cast out your name as evil, for the Son of man's sake. Rejoice ye in that day, . . . for, behold, your reward is great in heaven" (Luke 6:20-23).

Christ's pledge of a better tomorrow makes our todays bearable. Without His promises and presence, life would indeed be the cruel interruption of the peaceful state of nonexistence.

But His promise of future bliss does not mean there are no present blessings. His pledge of happiness in heaven is attested to by His gift of joy on earth. Meanwhile, He does not promise freedom from oppression, but endurance in spite of it. Not immunity from pain, but triumph over it. Not deliverance from heartache, but joy in suffering.

That is why Paul and Silas could sing while incarcerated, why John could rejoice on Patmos. And why we Christians can lustily sing:

> "Take the name of Jesus with you,
>   Child of sorrow and of woe;
>   It will joy and comfort give you,
>   Take it, then, where'er you go.
>
>   Precious name, O how sweet!
>   Hope of earth and joy of heaven;
>   Precious name, O how sweet!
>   Hope of earth and joy of heaven"
>   (*SDA Hymnal,* No. 474).

Christ heals us of our backsliding.

"I will heal their backsliding, I will love them freely: for mine anger is turned away from him" (Hosea 14:4).

Having declared our allegiance to Christ, we sometimes capitulate to evil, we surrender to soul-eroding forces of temptation. We are alerted in His Word against the love of the world "entering in," duly warned against the weeds that choke out the grain. But we sometimes err.

At times we become so busy earning a living that we neglect our own personal devotions. Sometimes we become so heavily engaged even in the service and mission of our church that we lose resolve and start to rely upon other means for success, deciding that there are more palatable routes to purity than the somber Beatitudes. We justify our actions by telling ourselves that these are merely small or temporary deviations. And we transgress.

Christ cautions us. He speaks to us. But He does not stop us in our flight from rectitude.

He watches sadly as we are pulled by the allurements of sin and pushed by the pain of hobbled hopes and soured relations. But He does not give up on us. He locates us in the pigpen of disobedience and points us back toward the Father's house. And we reply, "I will arise and go!"

We have often been shamed by our wounding Him afresh, and sometimes stigmatized by elder siblings "who never leave home." But we find healing again in the Father's love.

Christ heals us of our pride.

He whose heavy cross was lifted by another removes from our frail backs the crushing burden of self-redemption. Christ relieves us of the futility of carrying our achievements, our efforts, our personal successes, up the ladder of grace.

We so often forget that the government of our rescue is placed upon His sturdy shoulders. He has withstood the pressures of time and circumstance, and is the cornerstone of our salvation, the rock of our redemption, the "immovable mover" of our spiritual growth.

And that is a lesson that we learn in the crucible of daily experience, for just when we think we have "arrived" in faith, when we mistake the nature and source of our triumphs, Christ reminds us of our fallen condition, our utter dependence upon His, not our, works.

It is true that "the proud heart strives to earn salvation; but both our title to heaven and our fitness for it are found in the righteousness of Christ. The Lord can do nothing toward the recovery of man until, convinced of his own weakness, and stripped of all self-sufficiency, he yields himself to the control of God. Then he can receive the gift that God is waiting to bestow. From the soul that feels his need, nothing is withheld. He has unrestricted access to Him in whom all fullness dwells" *(The Desire of Ages,* p. 300).

Only those people who by constant refusal of His care sin against the Holy Ghost are denied Christ's help. He who heeded the centurion's plaintive request to heal his son, who saw the weeping Mary and Martha from afar, who had pity on the bereaved widow of Nain, also healed Matthew of his materialism, James and John of their resentment, Peter of His impetuosity, Thomas of His doubt, Paul of his haughtiness, and Nicodemus of his pride. And He can and does heal us. There is no weakness, no addiction, no habit, entrenched by time or sealed by indulgence, that is beyond His touch.

There is only one condition placed on His healing: we must sincerely desire it. That is the essence of His promise: "Return . . . , and I will heal your backslidings" (Jer. 3:22). Christ does not heal us arbitrarily or against our wills. Those whose hurts and diseases are healed are those who look to Him in hopeful faith.

Christ's healing was dramatically portrayed by the bronzed serpent that Moses erected above the dying Israelites. Bronze was a material of special value in ancient times. It represented wealth and beauty and endurance. The bronze serpent was therefore a stark contrast to the slithering creatures that infested the desert floor.

Jesus is like that. He was made "like unto" us (Heb. 2:17). Yet He was different, and that difference is His rich character, His perfect holiness, His righteous endurance.

It was the deadly serpents at their feet that poisoned the Israelites; it was the bronzed serpent raised up high that healed them. Those who believed and obeyed, those who dared look, were healed. We too must look up to a Source higher than ourselves. He has commanded: "Look unto me, and be ye saved, all the ends of the earth" (Isa. 45:22).

This Source to whom we look is one made "in the likeness of sinful flesh" (Rom. 8:3), but who was not sinful (1 Peter 1:19); one who "was in all points tempted like as we are, yet without sin" (Heb. 4:15).

"Likeness" is not sameness. His equipment, though like ours, was not sinful as is ours. How do we know that? We know because Christ was not born in sin and "shapen in iniquity" as are we (Ps. 51:5). His nature did not require conversion. He who healed others of their sins needed no such healing Himself.

True, in Gethsemane when He had taken on our sins, He needed an intercessor, but He never needed a healer. From the cradle to the grave, He retained the absolute holiness of His birth.

As the mob watched Him die they called out in derision, "He saved others; let him save himself, if he be Christ, the chosen of God" (Luke 23:35).

How cruel of them. How utterly ungrateful and heartless. How thankless! All His life He had worked in their behalf. Evidences of His healing abounded. There was no shortage of witnesses to His good deeds. But now these who had so recently shouted hosannas cried "Crucify Him!" and "If thou be the king of the Jews, save thyself" (verse 37).

No doubt He was tempted to do just that. Christ, as a human being, faced a double challenge: to resist the appeal to His human nature to retaliate and save Himself, and to resist the penchant of divinity to destroy transgressors. Of course, He could have saved Himself. He "could have called 10,000 angels."

But because Christ could not save Himself *and* us, He chose death. "With his stripes we are healed" (Isa. 53:5).

His life brought us healing. His death brought us forgiveness. His resurrection brought us life. His intercession brings us acceptance with the Father.

Christ's blood is the only antidote for our spiritual condition. Like healing herbs crushed for our physical ills, Christ was crushed for our benefit. He submitted Himself to the smiters. He took their blows and their curses. And His virtues, absorbed through prayer and meditation upon His Word, provide healing for our sin-sick souls.

The healing Word is the only cure for our chronic disease of sin. There are no "earthly medicines" sufficient for that task. Jesus alone is able. He is the light of our lives, the health of our souls, our balm in Gilead, our master physician.

Christ is our righteous sun of healing.

CHAPTER 12

CHRIST OUR RIGHTEOUS SANCTIFICATION

"But of him are ye in Christ Jesus, who of God is made unto us wisdom, and righteousness, and sanctification, and redemption" (1 Cor. 1:30).

Sanctification is holiness, the condition of acceptance with God; it is the state of being that renders us fit for fellowship with sinless beings in heaven and the earth made new. Christ is our righteous sanctification.

The concept of sanctification, it is apparent, has a prominent place in both Old and New Testament teachings. What is not so apparent is how so many obviously imperfect individuals, such as the members in Corinth (1 Cor. 1:2; 6:11) and those of Thessalonica (1 Thess. 5:27), deserve this description.

That paradox is resolved when we understand that there are, in reality, two types, or levels, of sanctification portrayed in the Word of God. The first is the sanctification of works, the daily maturing process, the constant flowering of the character toward the likeness of Christ, our model man.

This is the sanctification that is the "work of a lifetime" *(Christ's Object Lessons,* p. 65). It is the journey we begin when we first believe, and it never ends.

At our spiritual birth we were not very advanced in knowledge or works. But as time passed, we became much more developed in righteousness than when we first believed. As a result of our study of Scripture and our spiritual devotions, we have grown in faith and gained in righteousness. But we have not finished growing and gaining. We now, and as long as we live, must continue the fight for victory over ourselves.

The aftereffects of the fall of our ancestors in Eden are devastating. We humans have drifted so far from our original likeness to God, that the labor of the rest of our short lives would not be sufficient to equal His character—the standard for salvation. That is true in part because of the superior quality of His goodness, but also because of the inferior nature of our being.

In Eden we lost our innocence. But that wasn't all. The failure of our first parents plunged humanity to a lower spiritual level—we no longer possess our former sinless state. That in part is what Martin Luther meant when he wrote:

"The material itself is faulty. The clay, so to speak, out of which this vessel began to be formed is damnable. What more do you want? This is how I am; this is how all men are. Our very conception, the very growth of the fetus in the womb, is sin, even before we are born and begin to be human beings" *(Luther's Works,* vol. 12, p. 348).

Yes, we can and do overcome. But what is it that we Christians overcome?

Sin is what we overcome. But not simply the wrongful suggestions of Satan brought from *without.* It is also the never-ending stream of evil suggestions emanating from *within.* In this is the essence of Paul's postconversion confession: "I see another law in my members, warring against the law of my mind" (Rom. 7:23).

The fact that our minds never cease to conjure evil is evidence of the inbred evil with which we must wrestle daily. These sinful leanings, even though we resist and overcome them, display the critical difference between the nature of the progenitors of the human race before their fall in Eden and that which has burdened mankind since.

Thus, we are rescued, but always being restored; redeemed, but always recovering; converted, but always overcoming. And that is why absolute recovery from our state will be attained only when we corruptibles "put on incorruption" (1 Cor. 15:53).

Nevertheless, if we would be translated to heaven then, we must be transformed in His likeness now; that is, we must acquire the inclination for obedience that begins our journey back toward the perfection of our original nature.

The transformation and resulting enhancement effected in us is wondrous: our behavior is modified; our priorities are reset; our desires are reoriented.

But we are not upgraded to the level of Adam in his pre-Fall, sinless nature.

Yes, we can become victors over sin. But the desire to sin remains in us. It does not drive and control us as it did before our surrender to Christ, but it is the source of "never-ending contention." Our best efforts are stained with the marks of our humanity.

This very fact led Paul to write: "Not by works of righteousness which we have done, but according to his mercy he saved us" (Titus 3:5). And again: "By the deeds of the law there shall no flesh be justified" (Rom. 3:20).

We must never forget that "good works are but the result of the working of His sin-pardoning love. They are no credit to us, and we have nothing accorded to us for our good works by which we may claim a part in the salvation of our souls" *(Our High Calling,* p. 118).

That is why we must experience the second type, or level, of salvation—the sanctification of faith and peace, the unearned gift of Christ's righteousness—*His* sanctification. It is because "all our righteousnesses are as filthy rags" (Isa. 64:6) and "no man . . . sinneth not" (1 Kings 8:46) that He "is made unto us wisdom, and righteousness, and sanctification, and redemption" (1 Cor. 1:30).

That is how we who are being sanctified—being made holy—can claim to be already perfect (Heb. 10:14).

Vast and critical differences exist between our sanctification, which is wrought *in* us, and His sanctification, which He bestows *upon* us. These differ, for example, in *quality.*

Our sanctification is limited by our humanity. Christ's sanctification springs from the unstained nature of Him who became like us and who lived with us, but who needed neither conversion nor forgiveness. Christ did not have those internal leanings that suggest evil. He was not born at "enmity against God" (Rom. 8:7). There is mixed with His righteousness none of the sorrow for sin that necessarily accompanies ours. "Christ did not possess the same sinful, corrupt, fallen disloyalty we possess" *(Selected Messages,* book 3, p. 131).

Christ never needed personal justification because His absolute sanctification suffered no breach of loyalty.

Our sanctification and His sanctification differ also in *consequence.* Our sanctification—the sanctification that is imparted—is miraculous, but it is not comprehensive. It does not resolve our past, present, and future needs for cleansing.

On the other hand, His sanctification—the sanctification that is imputed—provides gives total coverage for our needs. It encompasses all the unconquered territory of our souls and is as effective at the surrender that marks conversion as it can or will be at any future time in our experience.

That sanctification that is imparted to us does not qualify us for heaven is witnessed to by the fact that the repentant thief at Calvary was saved without having engaged in Christian labors. He had no opportunity to visit nursing homes, pass out tracts, give Sabbath school offerings, sing in choirs, conduct Bible studies, or even to turn his back on Broadway's temptations. He had not developed sanctification.

What he did have, though, was imputed sanctification: Christ's robe that covered his undeveloped life and made him acceptable to God. He experienced the *passive righteousness* imputed to all whom Christ accepts, but not the *active righteousness* that is developed in our day-to-day living.

Another difference exists, and that is *focus.* Righteousness that is imparted speaks to "Christ in us." Its focus is our stature, our achievements, our progress in grace. Righteousness that is imputed speaks to "Christ over us." Its focus is Christ's achievement, His victorious life, His status with God.

Isaiah had this latter kind of righteousness in mind when he wrote: "I will greatly rejoice in the Lord, my soul shall be joyful in my God; for he hath clothed me with the garments of salvation, he hath covered me with the robe of righteousness, as a bridegroom decketh himself with ornaments, and as a bride adorneth herself with her jewels" (Isa. 61:10).

Jesus had both our sanctification and His in mind when He said: "For their sakes I sanctify myself, that they also might be sanctified" (John 17:19).

And there is a difference in *process.* Our sanctification is a process leading us from one degree of grace to another. It is growth, development.

Our sanctification is acquired through earnest expenditure of energy in the study of God's Word, self-denial as shown in fasting, witnessing and sharing, resisting temptation, and of course, quality time spent in prayer. Private prayer. Family prayer. Public prayer.

Paul, writing about the process of sanctification, chided his readers: "Ye have not yet resisted unto blood, striving against sin" (Heb. 12:4). Our sanctification consists of the daily wrestling, boxing, running, striving, pressing, that are enjoined upon us in the Word of God.

Hans LaRondelle described this growth-producing process well: "The apostolic concept of Christian sanctification is dynamic and progressive, constantly growing in the knowledge of God, and 'in the grace and knowledge of our Lord and Savior Jesus Christ' (2 Peter 3:18, NIV). But growth is not automatic, whether physical or spiritual. Spiritual growth, just as physical growth, is a matter of eating, drinking, and exercising" *(Christ Our Salvation,* p. 74).

The result of that process is a new way of living, one that demonstrates that our affections are "on things above" (Col. 3:2). That is what trains our thoughts for life in Paradise.

But Christ's sanctification, the righteousness that He imputes to us, contains none of our works. This is altogether from God. This sanctification is not gradual or progressive, and it is not amenable to improvement. It represents perfect obedience: the unimpeachable, unapproachable, unsurpassable righteousness of Christ, so impeccable that a thousand lifetimes would not be long enough for us to create it, and a myriad of millenniums would be too short to improve upon it. It is grace plus and minus nothing.

And it is all ours for the asking.

By simply wanting, confessing, and believing, we can have the sanctification of Christ. It is ours when in faith we turn away from ourselves and look to our Saviour in humble confession of our need.

Whereas we work to attain the sanctification that produces the *fruits of righteousness*; we simply believe to receive the sanctification that brings the *covering of righteousness.*

This we cannot earn. Christ has already earned it. It is already completed, wrought through the years of Christ's earthly experience, given to us without price, save our willingness to consecrate ourselves to Him.

And that is why our essential concern as Christians is different from that of all other religions. We know that we must strive toward the model of perfection, the life of Christ. We also know that the essence of our salvation, the nexus of our redemption, is not a goal, but a gift. The quintessential principle of our religion is not *what we must do,* but what *Christ has already done.*

Perhaps Paul presents the clearest difference between the sanctification that is imparted (i.e., produced within us) and that which is imputed (i.e., bestowed upon us) in Hebrews 10:10: "By the which will we are sanctified through the offering of the body of Jesus Christ once for all."

Amazing! The event is already ours. We have been sanctified!

And how? Through the sacrifice of the body of Christ. And how does the sacrifice of Christ's body effect our sanctification? It does so because His death satisfies the Father's anger toward sin and makes His will accessible to us, and His will includes our sanctification (John 17:19; Heb. 10:9, 10).

Some people believe that a distinct, uncluttered emphasis upon this latter class of sanctification—the objective, imputed, comprehensive, free gift of Christ—mutes our appreciation for the subjective, imparted daily growth that results from our relationship to Christ. This, however, is not the case for the believing, trusting children of God.

Such are inspired by the promise that "continual progress in knowledge and virtue is God's purpose for us. His law is the echo of His own voice, giving to all the invitation, 'Come up higher. Be holy, holier still.' Every day we may advance in perfection of Christian character" *(The Ministry of Healing,* p. 503).

Come up higher? Be holier still? Advance in perfection of Christian character?

Yes! That is altogether important because absolute holiness is our passport to glory. And it is altogether possible because those whom He "has made perfect" (imputed righteousness) are "those who are being made holy" (imparted righteousness) (Heb. 10:14, NIV).

Christ is our righteous sanctification.

WINDOWS ON
HIS PROTECTION

CHAPTER 13

CHRIST OUR RIGHTEOUS STRONGHOLD

"Return to the stronghold, you prisoners of hope. Even today I declare that I will restore double to you" (Zech. 9:12, NKJV).

A stronghold is a fortification that provides refuge and protection against an enemy. It is a structure in which one finds not only defense, but sustenance and assurance. Jesus is our righteous stronghold.

When God sent these encouraging words to His people through Zechariah, they had just begun settling back home after 70 years of exile in Babylon and later Media-Persia. The Temple, left devastated and plundered by Nebuchadnezzar, was in the process of being restored, and the Jews entertained hopes for a bright and prosperous future.

However, in the midst of their newfound joy came unexpected difficulties. First, proselyte Jews who had chosen to remain in Persia were protesting to their former captors the very need of the Temple and its ceremonies. And worse, their fledgling government was being threatened by the military might of Tyre to the north and Ashkelon, Gaza, and Epron on the south.

The Jews were no longer exiles, but they were ringed by the might of belligerent forces. Raiding parties were already violating their borders. Their expectations of freedom and prosperity seemed more and more a cruel hoax. The struggling nation needed another miracle of deliverance, another act of divine intervention.

It was in their fear and extremity that God spoke to them, promising that though Tyre had steeled itself with armament and was heaping "silver as the dust" and "fine gold as the mire of the streets" (Zech. 9:3), He would cast down that nation, along with militaristic rulers in Ashkelon, Gaza, Philista, and Ashdod.

God sealed His promise by saying to His people: "Turn . . . to the strong hold, ye prisoners of hope: even to day do I declare that I will render double unto thee" (verse 12).

And God did intervene in their behalf. One of the more memorable examples of this was the uncharacteristic act of Alexander the Great in sparing Jerusalem while wreaking havoc on the rest of the region, including Persia itself.

The plight and deliverance of Israel in their post-Exilic period is a forceful analogy of the spiritual salvation offered to us in Christ.

The essence of our condition is that we are all hemmed in by overwhelming forces of time and circumstance. We are all victims of a nature that tramples our hopes and dashes our choicest dreams. Hounded, harassed, harangued, we find ourselves overmatched by "all that is in the world, the lust of the flesh, and the lust of the eyes, and the pride of life" (1 John 2:16). Unable to break out of this ring of death, we remain prisoners—prisoners of hope, but prisoners nonetheless.

As the Jews were delivered from their exile in Persia, "the pit wherein is no water" (Zech. 9:11), so have we Christians been delivered from slavery to our wants, our unconverted state.

We were sinners, without hope, unsaved, unhappy, mired in the mud of transgression, stuck in the pit of filthy disobedience. We suffered the debility of unobstructed, unresisting disobedience. Life was empty then, disappointing and unfulfilling. We had only a hopeless end toward which to look—the light of truth had not penetrated our hearts.

But we heard the voice of Jesus calling. From high above our cells in the dungeon of sin, we heard that sweet voice and we believed. And when we did, He delivered us. By the provisions of "the blood covenant" sealed in heaven, typified in every altar sacrifice, ratified ultimately on Calvary, He freed us, not from the reality of the sinful nature with which we are destined to live until we mortals "put on immortality" (1 Cor. 15:53), but from its tyrannical control.

Our conversion changed our state from hirelings to heirs, from hopeless to hopeful.

But it did not insulate us from evil. We have not been placed beyond the continuous annoyances of our repressed but insistent evil nature. We are delivered from the pit of disobedience, but not from the perils of temptation or the defects of our organs of sensation, or the attacks of Satan, whose pent-up wrath against our inaccessible God so fiercely afflicts His people.

Are we, then, delivered to be devoured? released to be ravaged, unfettered to be undone? No! There is safety in Jesus. He is our hiding place, our city of refuge, our covert in the storm, our fortress and covering, our righteous stronghold.

In Bible days, strongholds were places of protection where soldiers and citizens alike might find safety. David spoke of such a refuge when he said: "Lead me to the rock that is higher than I. For thou hast been a shelter for me, and a strong tower from the enemy. . . . I will trust in the covert of thy wings" (Ps. 61:2-4).

Isaiah also had such a place in mind when he prophesied of Israel's peace, saying: "In that day shall this song be sung in the land of Judah; we have a strong city; salvation will God appoint for walls and bulwarks" (Isa. 21:1).

The more secure strongholds were protected not only by armed troops but by nature as well. Hence, the name "high tower" was given to those forts built on inaccessible hills overlooking bodies of water. But they were also known as "strong towers" because their wide moats and massive walls presented further difficulties for their enemies.

Christ is our impregnable stronghold.

To liken our Lord to a stronghold is to ascribe to Him a number of characteristics that are vital to our salvation. First and foremost is His *unassailableness*. Christ proved Himself to be morally unconquerable.

Had Christ never come to earth, He would have remained forever physically unassailable—but not morally. The accusation that Lucifer made against Him before the fall of Adam and Eve would have left His character in eternal doubt. But not now. By making Himself vulnerable in this world, He became invulnerable throughout the universe. He became assailable in time in order to be unassailable throughout eternity. He allowed Himself to be unprotected while dying so that we might be protected while living. That is how He became our stronghold.

Jeremiah celebrated this truth when he wrote: "Their Redeemer is strong; the Lord of hosts is his name: he shall thoroughly plead their cause, that he may give rest to the land" (Jer. 50:34).

Christ Himself referred to this provision in the parable of the man who proved stronger than the strong, who overcame the tyrant and divided his spoils (Luke 11:21, 22). The angels who ascended with our Lord emphasized His prowess as they shouted in response to the feigned curiosity of their heavenly counterparts: "The Lord strong and mighty, the Lord mighty in battle" (Ps. 24:8).

And that, in an inferior but accurate sense, is what Sir Walter Raleigh had in mind when he said: "My strength is as the strength of ten because my heart is pure." He is not righteous because He is strong; He is strong because He is righteous.

Christ is our available stronghold.

There were six cities, or strongholds, of refuge provided to Israel. These were located so as to ensure that no citizen was more than a half-day's journey from safety. The roads were kept in good repair, and signposts marked "Refuge" were strategically placed to guide the fleeing accused to safety. An individual who accidentally killed another person could run to any of these hiding places for protection.

Once behind the giant gates of the city, the avenging kin could trouble him no more. All threats of punishment were suspended when the fugitive entered the refuge. The hope of every desperate defendant was to enter such a stronghold of safety.

Even so, Jesus is our available stronghold. He is not an absentee landlord; He is nigh unto us, in Paul's words, "not far" (Acts 17:27). By His blood we are brought into the presence of God Himself (Eph. 2:13). He is a stronghold to whom we run and in whom we find acquittal and righteousness and peace. He is indeed "our refuge and strength, a very present help in trouble" (Ps. 46:1).

Faith drives us to this Stronghold, not fear.

Fear of Satan, fear of destruction, fear of suffering—fear even of hell itself—do not give legitimacy within the Stronghold. Those who come to Him must come in faith—faith that His absolute perfection and total holiness are accepted by the Father in the sinner's behalf; faith that His righteousness is abundantly available and altogether adequate; faith that the character of Christ provides our complete security; faith that the impregnability of the Strong Tower holds yesterday, today, and forever.

In the castle of His love, there is not just insurance against Satan's darts, but assurance of victorious living and, at last, life everlasting.

Christ is our necessary stronghold.

Our desperate need is for a moral stronghold. Satan is a tyrannical creditor who would extract our very lives. We owe him. We owe the law. We owe justice. The penalty is our annihilation, our everlasting nothingness. Our hope, our *only* hope, is the Stronghold, Jesus Christ.

Humans have, of course, built many false strongholds, high Babel-like towers, which rear themselves upon the landscape of our moral experience, but which are, in reality, fickle mirages, cruel constructs, fatal diversions from true happiness.

Fame is just such an apparition—and so is wealth and power. But the most cruel of all is works, *our* works. Herein is the greatest of all spiritual realities: Our works avail nothing in terms of salvation merits; Christ's works avail all.

Human accomplishments and sacrifices are pleasing to God, but they are not redemptive. The fruit of our relationship with Christ will be good works, but none of our works are good enough to earn heaven. That is why Solomon enjoined: "The name of the Lord is a strong tower; the [consistently] righteous man—upright and in right standing with God—runs into it and is safe, high [above evil] and strong" (Prov. 18:10, Amplified).

We are not righteous because we run; we are righteous because we are in the Tower, and only as long as the Tower engulfs us will we remain righteous. Outside the Tower we are victimized by the enemy, the hapless target of a foe much stronger than we are. If we would escape the avenger, we must drop our weight of prideful works and run in eager desperation to the safety that Christ's righteousness provides.

Christ is our beneficent stronghold.

The promise of our Saviour, given through Zechariah, is "I will render double unto thee" (Zech. 9:12). Between the capture of Jerusalem by Nebuchadnezzar and the return under Nehemiah and Zerubbabel, Israel had experienced some 70 years of joyless life. Whole generations were born and died knowing only oppression and the bleak longing for their home.

But then at last their fortunes were reversed. A new day dawned, and they moved from the parched pits of Babylon and Persia to the sunlit freedom of their rebuilt city. Bitterness was a thing of the past. Their fearful lesson of obedience and dependence upon Christ had been learned. It was then that God fulfilled through them what He had promised to their Father Abraham: blessings above all other nations and a prowess that made them a byword among the peoples of the earth. He gave them gladness for sorrow and the oil of joy for mourning.

No longer exiles, they flourished in might, in economy, in health, and in intellect. More significant, their nation served as the cradle for the long-promised Messiah. The privileges of their new relationship far exceeded in quantity and quality the weight of their captivity. They were, in spite of past relations and unpleasantries, still God's "firstborn."

As in their laws, a firstborn son of even an estranged wife was entitled to a double portion of the father's inheritance (Deut. 21:17), so were they beneficiaries of a love that transcended all deserving and expectation.

Our salvation is no less magnanimous.

With only our sordid past, filled with disappointment and disaffection, we stand as unclad Joshuas before the High Priest of our souls. With contrite hearts and bitter memories of broken promises, with inherited sinfulness and cultivated transgressions, we meekly confess: "Nothing in our hands we bring; simply to the cross we cling." And He who has punished us sorely rewards us doubly. He gives "beauty for ashes, the oil of joy for mourning, the garments of praise for the spirit of heaviness" (Isa. 61:3).

We receive double for our shame: double gratification, double satisfaction, double joy.

But our greatest shame is not the failures of yesteryear; it is the lack of faith today. It is our disposition to discount, to distrust, to doubt, the merits of Christ's righteousness. Zechariah's message has special meaning for our generation. We too are encompassed with superior odds, we too deserve none of His blessings, we too qualify for none of His goodness.

But when we flee to Him as a bird to the mountain, we discover in His hiding place acceptance and peace and everlasting joy.

Christ is our righteous stronghold.

CHAPTER 14

CHRIST OUR RIGHTEOUS STANDARD

"So shall they fear the name of the Lord . . . from the rising of the sun. When the enemy shall come in like a flood, the Spirit of the Lord shall lift up a standard. . . . The Redeemer shall come to Zion, and unto them that turn from transgression" (Isa. 59:19, 20).

A standard is a banner or flag that illustrates the special characteristics of an organization, an emblem that proclaims its identity and inspires its loyalties. Christ is our righteous standard.

As Christians we are His standard bearers, His loyal soldiers. As the early disciples went forth to witness, their attitude was summed up in this statement: "Christ's name was to be their watchword, their badge of distinction, their bond of union, the authority for their course of action, and the source of their success. Nothing was to be recognized in His kingdom that did not bear His name and superscription" *(The Acts of the Apostles, p. 28).*

The one characteristic that, more than any other, identifies Christ is holiness.

God is holy: "I the Lord your God am holy" (Lev. 19:2). His location is holy (Eze. 20:40). His city is holy (Rev. 21:2). His temple is holy (Hab. 2:20). His name is holy (Lev. 22:2).

How holy is God? He is so holy that He radiates light; He emanates energy. He is so pristinely pure that He shines. He is so righteous that He illuminates the galaxies with the brilliance of His character. He is so holy that anything sinful is instantly cremated in His presence, completely done away with. "The Lord thy God is a consuming fire," wrote Moses (Deut. 4:24).

God is so holy that the ground shook when He occupied the mountain and thundered to His people. He is so holy that the meekest man who ever lived could see only His afterglow—and not His face. He is so holy that the high priest ministered before the Shekinah with bells suspended from his garments and a rope about his waist so that if, because of sin in his life, he was stricken before God's presence and the bells ceased ringing, his associates could remove his body without risking death themselves before the purity of His presence.

How holy is the Lord? He is so holy that when the Philistines placed the captured ark in their temple, their god Dagon was discovered facedown, with only the trunk intact, and the people were smitten with boils (1 Sam. 5:3-6).

How holy is God? He is so holy that the six-winged seraphim cover their feet and their faces as they bend low before His throne. He is so holy that the 24 elders and the living creatures spend all their days crying, "Holy, Holy, Holy, Lord God Almighty. . . . Thou art worthy, O Lord, to receive glory and honour and power" (Rev. 4:8-11).

And when He came to this earth, He brought to Bethlehem's manger the condensed essence of His eternal righteousness. The angels spoke joyfully to Mary of "that holy thing which shall be born of thee" (Luke 1:35).

Christ, whose pristine purity lit the heavenly bodies, abdicated His office but not His holiness. But for our sakes He hid the brightness of His being. He muted the manifestations of His purity, for we could not have withstood the glow of His presence.

Perhaps the poet George Herbert came as close as anyone in describing that event when he wrote:

> "The power of God as He did ride
>   In His majestic robes of glory,
>   Resolved to light, and so one day
>   He did descend, undressing all the way.
>   The stars, His attire of light . . . obtained
>   The cloud His bow, the fire, His spear,
>   The sky, His azure mantle gained;
>   And when they asked what He would wear,
>   He smiled and said as He did go,
>   He had new clothes a-making here below.
>   'The Word became flesh.'"

That is where the greater victory was won. It was one thing to be the holy Son of God, adored by angels, praised by the Father, engulfed in the antiseptic atmosphere of heaven—and another to be Son of man on earth, "despised and rejected" by the multitude.

Satan understood that and fought Christ relentlessly: he sent lawyers to entrap Him, rabbis to harass Him, demons to torment Him. The devil himself tried Him mercilessly from the cradle to the grave in an effort to overwhelm Him, but Christ did not fail or become discouraged. In His mouth was found no guile. He did no violence nor deceit. "In His human nature He maintained the purity of His divine character" *(My Life Today,* p. 323).

Jesus overcame destructive emotions, unhealthy appetites, all stimuli to excess, each desire to neglect, every temptation to self-exultation and retaliation that ruminates in the human mind. He maintained the absolute character perfection in which He was born.

Christ committed no error, nor did He omit any good. He passed all the tests and was able of His victory to say, "The prince of this world cometh, and hath nothing in me" (John 14:30).

That quality of holiness is our goal—our standard of achievement. His command is "Be ye holy; for I am holy" (1 Peter 1:16). We are called to be "servants to righteousness unto holiness" (Rom. 6:19), putting on "the new man, which after God is created in righteousness and true holiness" (Eph. 4:24). This holiness is a nonnegotiable prerequisite of salvation.

Humans were made to take the place of fallen angels, and while God's plan has been delayed by sin, He fully intends to carry it through. However, He cannot, He will not, replace sinful angels with sinful humans. He is perfectly holy and will accept from us "nothing but purity and holiness; one spot, one wrinkle, one defect in character, will forever debar [us] from heaven, with all its glories and treasures" *(Testimonies,* vol. 2, p. 453).

That is why we must be saved *from* our sins, not *in* our sins. That is why we are reminded: "The stamp of character, with the disposition of obedience acquired at the new birth, is the only contribution that we can take to the new world" *(Sanctuary and Perfection,* p. 129).

No wonder Paul speaks of our journey as a "heavenly calling" (Heb. 3:1), a "holy calling" (2 Tim. 1:9), a "high calling of God in Christ Jesus" (Phil. 3:14). Clearly, it is, as Jesus taught, a narrow way that leads to everlasting life (Matt. 7:14).

The righteousness we have described thus far is a goal, a mark toward which we must strive. But the paradox of it all is that it is not the goal of righteousness that saves; it is the gift of righteousness that Christ bestows. It is His gift of *imputed* righteousness that qualifies us for eternal life.

We need the *gift* of righteousness because we never fully accomplish the *goal* of righteousness. Because "we cannot equal the pattern" *(Testimonies,* vol. 2, p. 549), we must be "partakers of *his* holiness" (Heb. 12:10; italics supplied).

But before we can desire the merits of His life, we must discern the true quality of His goodness. Before we can appreciate His priceless gift, we must grasp the magnitude of His holiness.

Our failure to do this is, perhaps, the real reason we sometimes have such high hopes for our own goodness and such slight concern for His gift. It is when we turn our eyes from lesser attractions and see Christ, as did Isaiah, high and lifted up, that we are impacted by both the high *calling* and high *costing* of our salvation.

That is possible because, "having brought conviction . . . and presented before the mind the *standard* of righteousness, the Holy Spirit withdraws the affections from the things of this earth and fills the soul with a desire for holiness" *(The Acts of the Apostles,* pp. 52, 53; italics supplied).

How well have we appreciated the holiness aspect of Christ's character? The evidence suggests: not well enough.

How do we know? By the alarming lack of respect that some people have toward the things of God: His name, His church, His sanctuary. We know by the blatant disregard for the prophet Habakkuk's sober demand: "The Lord is in his holy temple: let all the earth keep silence before him" (Hab. 2:20).

No doctrine of the church has orthodoxy without this holiness.

With Christ's holiness, baptism is a commemoration of His death, burial, and resurrection. Without Christ's holiness, it is a ritual introduction to a life of frustrated activity in the body of believers. With Christ's holiness, judgment is the successful vindication of our character wrought by our righteous Advocate. Without Christ's holiness, it is deserved condemnation by our relentless accuser. With Christ's holiness, stewardship is our reasonable response to our purchase by His blood. Without Christ's holiness, it is vain effort, empty works, unprofitable penance.

With Christ's holiness, the Second Coming is the "blessed hope" of those people whose dependence upon His righteousness gives them justifiable expectation to stand safely in the blazing presence of God the Father. Without an adequate view of Christ's holiness, it is the anxious and illogical certainty of those whose trust in their own accomplishments mutes the value of the earthly victories of God the Son.

It is when we uplift Christ's holiness in this manner that we fulfill Jeremiah's stirring call: "Set up the standard upon the walls of Babylon, make the watch strong, set up the watchmen, prepare the ambushes. . . . Set ye up a standard in the land, blow the trumpet among the nations" (Jer. 51:12-27). It is when we uplift Him that we heed Isaiah's urgent cry: "Go through, go through the gates; prepare ye the way of the people; cast up, cast up the highway; gather out the stones; lift up a standard for the people" (Isa. 62:10).

Thus, we remind ourselves and our public that time has not diminished God's glory; that He still demands of the people of earth a Creator/creature relationship; that the enemy of all righteousness, who once offered kingdoms that he did not own in exchange for worship that he did not deserve, is the author of Babylon's confusion; that God's holiness is His glory, His imprimatur, His standard by which He distinguishes Himself—and underneath which He rallies and protects His people.

The cry of the first angel to fear, glorify, and worship God is a call to earth's last dwellers to respect His holiness (Rev. 14:7). The warning of the second angel that it is apostasy to claim His name and not obey His Word is also an appeal to holiness (verse 8). And the third angel's promise of destruction to all those who persist in disobedience is likewise a call to holy living before the holy God (verses 8-12).

John summarizes the holiness aspect of the angels' decrees by saying: "Who will not fear you, O Lord, and bring glory to your name? For you alone are holy. All nations will come and worship before you, for your righteous acts have been revealed" (Rev. 15:4, NIV).

Could it be that the preaching of holiness as a component of Christ's righteousness is the weak or missing link in our doctrinal expositions?

We must not leave this critical function to other denominations or to dissident groups among us. Nor can we allow our personal struggles with temptation to mute this vital emphasis. The knowledge of our own humanity must not intimidate or deter us from lifting high the standard of holiness.

Each of Israel's 12 tribes camped and marched under an identifying banner. These banners were rallying points in times of battle, signaling hope and protection for the wounded in war. They were also beacons of hope for wayfaring strangers and ensigns of terror to their enemies.

Tradition suggests that each tribe had etched on its banner the logo of its fathers' house—a lion for Judah, a deer for Naphtali, a serpent for Dan, an eagle for Ephraim, the face of a man for Manasseh, etc. And very important, below each logo was listed all the major battles in which the tribe had fought and won.

We too have a banner that distinguishes our pilgrimage. On it is inscribed, as it was upon Aaron's miter and as it will be upon the heads of the redeemed: "HOLINESS TO THE LORD" (Ex. 39:30).

Even now we must lift up this banner, stained with blood and etched with the cross. We must raise it high. We must dare to unfurl its colors even in this age of spiritual indifference.

We must lift it up and advertise Christ's stellar triumphs at Bethlehem, in the Temple, in the wilderness, at Lazarus' burial site, in Pilate's judgment hall, in Gethsemane, before the Sanhedrin, on Mount Calvary, and at the entrance of

Joseph's new tomb.

But since He is *our* captain, *our* hero, *our* leader in battle, these victories are not just His—"His victory is ours" *(The Desire of Ages,* p. 123). And when we remain prostrate before the cross, "holiness has nothing more to require" *(Christ's Object Lessons,* p. 163).

It is by that realization that we are impelled to worship, empowered to obey, and emboldened to ever proclaim His name.

Christ is our righteous standard.

CHAPTER 15

CHRIST OUR RIGHTEOUS SHEPHERD

"I am the good shepherd: the good shepherd giveth his life for the sheep" (John 10:11).

A shepherd is a friend and custodian to nature's most celebrated symbol of naivety—sheep. The constant care that sheep require evidences their weaknesses and establishes for them and the shepherd a loving, lasting relationship. Jesus is our righteous shepherd.

Bible writers frequently compared believers to sheep. Ezekiel called God's people "sheep that wandered all through the mountains" (Eze. 34:6), "sheep that are scattered" (verse 12), sheep that are "prey to the heathen" (verse 28). Isaiah saw them as sheep that "have gone astray" (Isa. 53:6). Jeremiah, speaking of their vulnerability, typified them as sheep whose "shepherds have caused them to go astray" (Jer. 50:6). And the psalmist, seeing the sheep sinful and dying, asked of God, "Why doth thine anger smoke against the sheep of thy pasture?" (Ps. 74:1).

Christ Himself utilized this analogy in the tender shepherd/sheep imagery of John 10:1-8.

Christ is our provider.

Jesus said that He provides for His sheep. As their provider He supplies for them (1) the door (verse 7); (2) the call (verse 8); (3) the pasture (verse 9); and (4) the more abundant life (verse 10). These meanings are instructive.

Christ provides for us a door. By the analogy of the door, we are reminded that Christ is the only legitimate entrance to eternal life, our only possible way to restoration and fellowship with the Father. John quoted Him to have said: "I am the door: by me if any man enter in, he shall be saved" (verse 9). Luke wrote it another way: "For there is none other name under heaven given among men, whereby we must be saved" (Acts 4:12).

God is a "jealous God" (Ex. 20:5), a God whose hatred for sin dooms our wayward world, but whose great love rescues us individually. The door of reentry is Christ. Humans *can* gain favor again. We are not lost forever. There *is* acceptance back into the family of God, but only through the Son.

That which bars us from divine acceptance is the high standard of absolute righteousness. We cannot enter in because of our imperfect status. Unfinished holiness, no less than abject sinfulness, is a deterrent to eternal fellowship with God. But Jesus is our door to acceptance. It is His earned holiness that qualifies us for life in the Father's house.

The door to eternity must be unstained and unscarred by temporal dross. Had Christ failed in any way, had He succumbed to any temptation, He would have been disqualified as our way of transition, our point of entry into heavenly favor. But He stood every test; He passed all inspections. Thus, He is qualified to be our righteous shepherd.

Christ provides for us a call. By the analogy of "the call," we are reminded of the distinctiveness of Christ's relation to His people. Thieves and mercenaries may call, but they are not followed by sheep whose allegiance is to their Shepherd only. But the true Shepherd calls, and they hear. He calls His sheep en masse, and He calls them individually.

Christ's voice is duplicated by no other. His call is pronounced; it alone resonates with the sheep. Christ the righteous shepherd calls continually. He calls us by the moving upon the heart of the Holy Spirit. He calls us by the wisdom of the Word. He calls us through the arrangements of circumstances in our lives.

Ours is a world of many voices.

There are voices of doom and despair, voices of doubt and dismay, voices of cynicism and censure, voices of anger and arrogance, voices of materialism and mayhem. But above the din of life's confused concerns, Jesus calls. He calls to repentance, to purity; He calls to a higher state of obedience, to service, to commitment, to sacrifice.

In the words of Fannie Crosby's appealing song, treasured by so many through the years:

> "Jesus is tenderly calling thee home—
>   Calling today, calling today;
>   Why from the sunshine of love wilt thou roam,
>   Farther and farther away?
>   Calling today, calling today,
>   Jesus is calling, is tenderly calling today."

What makes His call so distinctive is His righteousness.

The authenticity of Christ's call is grounded in the singularity of His life: His overcoming sin in the flesh that bore the burdens of 4,000 years of human ills. He calls not as a potentate who, from the security of His throne, orders us to victory; He calls as one who has been tried and proven. Christ trod the way before us; He cleared away the underbrush; He successfully blazed the trail. He knows the way, and when He calls, we believe, we take courage, we follow.

We know that He has tested the footing ahead, and that gives us reassurance. He calms our doubts and soothes our fears, and we trust Him when we cannot trace Him. He is our righteous shepherd.

Christ provides for us pastures. By the analogy of the "pastures," we are reminded of His provisions for our spiritual sustenance. So vital a function of our salvation is this that God's people are called the "sheep of his pasture" (Ps. 100:3) and the "people of his pasture" (Ps. 95:7).

In this world there are other feeding grounds, other places in which sustenance may be found, but none like the pastures of the Righteous Shepherd, who allows us to recline in "green pastures" (Ps. 23:2), who feeds us in "good" and "fat" pastures (Eze. 34:14).

God's Word is the pasture in which His people gain the strength to live godly each day. It is the source of our vitality, the wellspring of our joy, the fount of our energy. From its consumption, we derive the vitamins of spiritual prowess that produce the rich fruits of righteousness.

The Word that "was made flesh and dwelt among us" (John 1:14), the Flesh that was transformed again to divinity, is compressed onto the pages of Scripture. It is a righteous Word made possible by a righteous Saviour. His purity stands out on every page. His holiness is exalted in every account. His perfection shines forth from every chapter and verse, illuminating the dark corners of our hearts, calling us to repentance.

The pristine righteousness of Christ's character is the focus of the Old Testament, the priests of which walked in fearful dread of stain as they ministered before the altar. And the purity of Christ's character is the highlight of the New Testament, the pages of which repeat again and again the victory of the God/Man, Jesus Christ.

Our strength for victory comes from Christ. In His pleasant pastures we find will and power for overcoming. He is our righteous shepherd.

Christ provides for us life more abundantly. By the promise of "life more abundantly," we are reminded of the superior joys of the life of obedience.

Satan's promise to confer on Eve added knowledge (Gen. 3:5) typifies all of his falsehoods. His agenda is destruction, seduction, and denigration of the human race. He it is who "climbeth up some other way, the same is a thief and a robber" (John 10:1).

Satan came to lessen us. His every effort is always to convince us to settle for "something less."

But Christ, the good shepherd, came that we might experience "something more, much more."

When the righteous Shepherd's spotless purity is sought and bestowed, we receive the presence of the Holy Spirit, and with it peace of mind. Our lives are lengthened, our days are gladdened, and we "ride upon the high places of the earth" (Isa. 58:14). Christ always provides more: more health, more happiness, more wisdom, more understanding, more patience, more exhilarating faith, more productive living, more godly acts, more purity and holiness. Christ is our righteous provider.

Christ is our protector.

The second major role that Christ ascribes to Himself is that of protector (John 10:11-15).

Sheep are very vulnerable to the ravages of weather, they are notably susceptible to disease, they are almost defenseless against predatory foes. Sheep need protection. Their health and survival demand not just the provisions already considered, but often the physical defense and personal sacrifice of the shepherd.

"He that is an hireling," John wrote, "and not the shepherd, . . . seeth the wolf coming, and leaveth the sheep, and fleeth" (John 10:12). Hired help and mercenaries flee before danger. False shepherds save themselves in the face of severe challenge. But the "good shepherd giveth his life for the sheep" (verse 10).

Christ effected our defense and deliverance upon the tree. His magnanimity is exceeded only by His sinlessness, and it is that which rendered His sacrifice acceptable to the Father.

The shepherd observes the elements and delivers the flock from the storms by leading them to alcoves of safety. Christ, our righteous shepherd, does not drive His sheep; He leads them. In the searing heat of life's desert experiences, He provides coverts for His flock. He Himself is as "the shadow of a great rock in a weary land" (Isa. 32:2). He leads us to the secret place of the Most High, where we are protected from spiritual disaster. He leads us beside still waters, where we are refreshed from living streams. He leads us to the church, His fold, where He is the head and where, banded together, we find comfort and mutuality.

And that is the message of J. H. Gilmore's hymn:

"He leadeth me! O blessed thought!
O words with heavenly comfort fraught!
Whate'er I do, wher'er I be,
Still 'tis God's hand that leadeth me."

The Good Shepherd knows His sheep by name and temperament, and discriminates between the fat and the lean, the weak and the strong. And if the strong take advantage of the weak, He will correct the aggressor and encourage the lesser. He who protects from destruction from without is also a defense against injustice within. He sees our motives and observes our strivings, and He judges among us, offering His own example of humility as our conscience against exercising lordship and unjust authority.

The Good Shepherd is always tender with the weak and feeble, gathering the young lambs in His bosom and gently leading them that are with young (Isa. 40:11).

A shepherd protects the flock against disease by isolating infectious sheep, those with distemper and communicable ills. The Good Shepherd does so by discipline and censure, and when necessary, by removing from the body of believers those elements that would weaken and destroy.

And as a shepherd washes his sheep, cleaning away the filth and grime accumulated in their journey, so Christ, the righteous shepherd, cleanses His flock by the application of His blood to the record of our sins. That is why John addressed the churches by saying: "Grace and peace to you from him who is, and who was, and who is to come, . . . from Jesus Christ, who is the faithful witness, the first-born from the dead. . . . To him who loves us and has freed us from our sins by his blood" (Rev. 1:4, 5, NIV).

Christ is our presenter.

The third role that Christ ascribes to Himself is that of presenter. The shepherd's duties do not end with protecting and providing for the sheep. The shepherd must at the end of the day, or the end of the journey, or the end of the season, or even at the end of his life, give an account to the owner.

This is true also with Christ. It is true first of all in the cosmic sense. Our world is that one lost sheep that left the fold, the rescue of which was accomplished by our loving Lord. No other would-be savior could suffice. Only the supremely righteous Christ could penetrate constellations and galaxies to reach and rescue our fallen world.

It is true also in the personal sense. Our Shepherd is responsible for preparing us individually for presentation to God. We who are not worthy of God's presence—we who, no matter how hard we try and how long we strive, can never qualify for fellowship with God—are nevertheless made presentable by Christ. He presents us to the Father free of "spot, or wrinkle, or any such thing" (Eph. 5:27) by clothing us with His righteous robe.

Paul explained this well in Romans 5:10: "For if, when we were enemies, we were reconciled to God by the death of his Son, much more, being reconciled, we shall be saved by his life."

His righteous life is not a promise of indiscriminate acceptance or covering of evil. No one who is presented to the Father can be guilty of unconfessed, unconquered sin. Christ's robe does not cover iniquity, but it does cover the unholy flesh of the suppliant sheep, who, while growing in grace, petition and receive the merits of His life.

And He who knows us by name will present us by name.

The redeemed will not be an aggregate mass, an indistinguishable crowd. We will be known there as we are known here, as individuals. From Adam to the least of the Shepherd's flock, we will be glorified; that is, immortalized to sinless perfection by Christ our righteous presenter.

Christ is our prevailer.

Last, Christ is our prevailer. His testimony is: "Therefore doth my Father love me, because I lay down my life, that I might take it again. No man taketh it from me, but I lay it down of myself. I have power to lay it down, and I have power to take it again. This commandment have I received of my Father" (John 10:17).

Shepherds do not always prevail. Some are outflanked and outwitted by marauding beasts, others are destroyed by the violence of nature, and still others are overcome by robbers and thieves. Sheep are sometimes victimized by the death of the shepherd, slain in their defense.

But while earthly shepherds do not always prevail, our righteous shepherd does.

For Him was fulfilled the prophet's cry: "Awake, O sword, against my shepherd, and against the man that is my fellow, . . . smite the shepherd, and the sheep shall be scattered" (Zech. 13:7). But Calvary was not terminal—it was tactical. His bleeding heel was bruised in death, but the bruiser's head was crushed by the perfection of His offering.

The jury held its verdict just long enough for the Defendant to rest from the trials of His life of suffering and sacrifice. On the preparation day He was the antitype, fulfilling 4,000 years of our expectation. On the holy Sabbath day He tasted the sleep that is the lot of all mortals. But on the third day He rose.

Flesh that had not experienced transgression would not know deterioration. The resurrection was the universal and everlasting vindication of His sinless life. He had prevailed over temptation. He had prevailed over pain. Now He prevailed over death and hell and Satan and the grave. Hear Him exclaim as He exited the darkness, "I am the resurrection and the life!"

No stronger testimony is available or necessary. He who provides, protects, and presents has also prevailed.

Christ is our righteous shepherd.

Windows on His Passion

CHAPTER 16

CHRIST OUR RIGHTEOUS SIN BEARER

"Therefore will I divide him a portion with the great, and he shall divide the spoil with the strong; because he hath poured out his soul unto death: and he was numbered with the transgressors; and he bare the sin of many, and made intercession for the transgressors" (Isa. 53:12).

A sin bearer is a being on whom the guilt of someone else is placed, one who accepts not only the guilt of others but also the consequences of their transgressions, thus making the punishment of the true offender unnecessary. Christ is our righteous sin bearer.

God hates sin, all sin. Big sins and little sins, public sins and private sins, old sins and new sins, sins against ourselves and sin against others, the sins of the youth and the sins of the elderly, weekday sins and Sabbath sins, sins of omission and sins of commission. God hates sin!

Why? Because sin is contrary to the high and holy character of God. Sin is rebellion against God. Sin is disrespect for God. Sin is ingratitude to God. Sin is arrogance before God. Sin is meanness toward God. Sin is tension with God. Sin is infectious; hence, dangerous to others and lethal to the individual bearer.

Each sin committed has dual consequences for its victim.

First, there are the immediate or natural consequences, the negative effects of actions that are incompatible with our physical and spiritual being. An example of such a sin is the use of tobacco. It is an act against nature for which we pay in predictable results: cancer, heart disease, emphysema, among others.

Consequences of such sins, enforced by the law of cause and effect, are capsulated in the solemn decree: "Whatsoever a man soweth, that shall he also reap" (Gal. 6:7). Planting the seeds of transgression ensures a harvest of pain.

But in addition to its natural results, sin has a second consequence, the judicial wrath, or punishment, from God.

Paul warned of this consequence when he wrote: "To them who by patient continuance in well doing seek for glory and honour and immortality, eternal life: but unto them that are contentious, and do not obey the truth, but obey unrighteousness, indignation and wrath, tribulation and anguish, upon every soul of man that doeth evil, of the Jew first, and also of the Gentile" (Rom. 2:7-9).

Furthermore, added Paul, "the wages of sin is death" (Rom. 6:23).

The Holy God is pledged to attack sin, not simply to wound it. He will rid the universe of its presence. He will annihilate not just sin, with its meanness and uncleanness, but also the people in whom this defiance is found.

Jesus knew that we could not survive the judicial consequences of transgression. He knew that our sentence was lethal, that we could not avert the "sting of death." So He pledged to take our sins, to suffer in our place.

This pledge is the thrilling core of the Baptist's cry: "Behold the Lamb of God, which taketh away the sin of the world" (John 1:29)! It is what the beloved John meant when he wrote: "He is the propitiation for our sins: and not for our's only, but also for the sins of the whole world" (1 John 2:2).

It is also what Ellen G. White had in mind when she wrote: "It is for thee that the Son of God consents to bear this burden of guilt; for thee He spoils the domain of death, and opens the gates of Paradise. He . . . offers Himself upon the cross as a sacrifice, and this from love to thee. He, the Sin Bearer, endures the wrath of divine justice, and for thy sake becomes sin itself" *(The Desire of Ages,* pp. 755, 756).

It was at Bethlehem that He became our sin bearer in the biological sense. As Mary's Son, Christ willingly encumbered Himself with the heavy burden of transgression, accepting a physical body that bore the natural consequences of 4,000 years of sin.

But it was not until the experience in the Garden of Gethsemane that He became our sin bearer in the judicial sense. For it was there that He was made sin for us.

Prior to Gethsemane, Christ functioned most pervasively as our "light bearer." John called Him the "light [that] shineth in darkness," the "true Light, which lighteth every man that cometh into the world" (John 1:5, 9).

All during His ministry on earth He functioned as a partner with His Father. Christ was always certain of His Father's pleasure, secure in God's presence and pleasure. The early realization that He experienced while beholding the Temple rites, the confirmation that He received at His baptism at Jordan, the reassurance He was given on the Mount of Transfiguration, the constant affirmations evidenced in His many miracles, all permitted Him to say: "I and my Father are one" (John 10:30).

But Gethsemane changed all that.

Until Gethsemane, Christ had functioned not only as hero of the people but as the prototype of sinless humanity. But when He entered into the Garden of

Gethsemane, He who at Bethlehem took off His royal robes and strapped on human garb pulled over that perfect humanity our sins and imperfections. He became sin for us, and was thus separated from the Father, who hates sin and promised to punish it wherever it exists.

In the Garden of Eden, sin separated the Father from His sinful creatures. In the Garden of Gethsemane, sin separated the Father from His sin-covered Son. For the first time the Members of the Godhead were at odds with Themselves; They were on opposite sides. In Gethsemane, Jesus moved from sunshine to shadow, from partner to enemy, from family to foe, from the pleasure of God's smile to the awesomeness of His frown upon sin.

"Christ was now standing in a different attitude from that in which He had ever stood before. . . . The sins of men weighed heavily upon Christ, and the sense of God's wrath against sin was crushing out His life" *(The Desire of Ages,* pp. 686, 687).

Every sin ever committed, accompanied by its sense of guilt, was placed upon Him. The pressure was so great that He became traumatized by unthinkable, unspeakable, unimaginable sorrow. His sinless yet human system was so jolted, His being so crushed, that His features were "disfigured beyond that of any man and His form marred beyond human likeness" (Isa. 52:14, NIV).

Satan had anticipated this moment. He knew its significance. He realized that if Christ were made to retreat from His mission, "the human race would be forever in his power" *(The Desire of Ages,* p. 687). Therefore, he heightened and quickened the drama, hoping that the crushing weight of human iniquity would intimidate Christ into retaliating against His persecutors, or abandoning His mission, or perhaps even saving Himself by the use of divine energies and thus disqualifying Himself to be our redeemer.

The pressure upon Christ became so great that His "sweat was as it were great drops of blood falling down to the ground" (Luke 22:44). There was no one to help Him, no shoulder to comfort, no hand to hold. Christ clung to the cold, hard ground, forgotten by His sleeping disciples, unprotected from the vengeful God.

"I have trodden the winepress alone," He said, "and of the people there was none with me" (Isa. 63:3).

God unsheathed His sword of justice upon His own dear Son, and from the pale, quivering lips of Jesus there came the anguished cry: "O My Father, if it be possible, let this cup pass from me" (Matt. 26:39).

Three times He pleaded for relief and mercy. Three times he cried for help. And at last His Father responded. God sent an angel messenger, the heavenly being who stood nearest to God, who had taken the place of the fallen Luther. He cradled our suffering Sin Bearer, reminding Him of His Father's love, reaffirming the necessity of His suffering for our salvation.

Jesus was revived, but the pain was not removed. His depression was lifted, but the storm had not abated. Given courage by the angel, He now awakened His sleeping disciples and turned to meet the advancing mob.

And that began the second phase of His sin-bearing experience.

In Gethsemane the pain of separation had gripped His soul, but now, before His accusers, it was the pain of humiliation that He felt. Christ was derided and denigrated, misquoted and maligned, slandered and spat upon, queried and accused. Before Annas and Caiaphas and Pilate and Herod and back to Pilate, He was dragged like a guilty animal, victimized by the greatest miscarriage of justice that the world has ever known.

Among the many rules of Hebrew jurisprudence violated by His captors were: (1) the law requiring a 72-hour notice for all such trials, (2) the law prohibiting trials at night, (3) the law prohibiting trials on the preparation day, (4) the law prohibiting false witnesses, (5) the law prohibiting false accusations, (6) the law prohibiting self-incrimination, (7) the law forbidding the high priest to deface His garments, (8) the law requiring that sentence be withheld until all evidence is given, and (9) the law permitting witnesses for the defendant.

There were no witnesses for the defense!

Just think of the many persons Christ had healed who would have gladly testified on His behalf. They could have asked the man born blind, whose eyes He had opened. They could have found the woman healed of a bleeding disorder. They could have interviewed the widow of Nain, the centurion and his son, Peter's mother-in-law, former lepers and demoniacs, Bartimaeus, Lazarus—literally a cast of thousands.

But He had no one to speak on His behalf, no character witnesses. After all He had done for others, there was no one to testify for Him.

But the worst injustice of all was the verdict of guilty in the face of obvious innocence. After Pilate had examined Jesus he addressed the chief priests: "Take ye him, and crucify him: for I find no fault in him" (John 18:6). Christ was pronounced guiltless, but nevertheless, condemned to die!

But that is how He became our sin bearer. Mark records: "And with Him they crucified two robbers, one on [His] right hand and one on His left. And the scripture was fulfilled which says, He was counted among the transgressors" (Mark 15:27, 28, Amplified).

Satan himself led the mob in search of Jesus. Satan led the jurors in their miscarriage of justice. And Satan orchestrated His death, the third and final stage of His sin-bearing experience, a painful execution.

Executions were carried out in many forms in Christ's day. Among them were drowning, stoning, decapitation, and of course, the most cruel and feared of all—crucifixion. In crucifixion several factors contributed to the death of the victim. Among them were exposure to the elements, physical shock, and slow, agonizing suffocation. The latter occurred as the body gradually sagged against the restraints, compressing the lungs and making breathing more and more diffi-cult. Usually, by the third day the prisoner, gasping painfully for air with what lit-tle energy was left, could strain no more and died the lonely, shameful death of the cross.

When it was desired that a person should die quicker, the custom was that the legs be broken. In the case of Christ, however, under the time constraints of the approach of the Sabbath, during which no one could be left hanging, a spear was thrust deep into His side. But He was already dead.

That act proved that "it was not the pain of the cross that caused the death of Jesus. . . . He died of a broken heart. His heart was broken by mental anguish. He was slain by the sin of the world" *(The Desire of Ages,* p. 772).

By His suffering, our sins were thoroughly excised, completely expiated, our propitiation total and eternal, our way to eternal life assured. Jesus died our sec-ond death.

But there is another benefit that accrued. By His death our righteousness was made possible: "Our sins were laid on Christ, punished in Christ, put away by Christ, in order that His righteousness might be imputed to us, who walk not after the flesh, but after the Spirit" *(Signs of the Times,* May 30, 1895).

Christ was not a transgressor, but He was "counted" one in His role as sin bearer. We are not righteous, but because of His goodness we are "counted" so, and thus we are qualified for heaven.

Our salvation requires more than our forgiveness. It also requires holiness, absolute, total perfection.

That for us is as impossible to attain as is the self-expiation of our sins. He who knew that we could not recover from the finality of death also knew that we could not attain the level of holiness required to avoid that punishment. That is why He died: to forgive us of our transgressions and to make His perfection available to us.

Christ fell beneath the mountain of sins He assumed in order to release to us the ocean of righteousness He earned. From that inexhaustible supply, we receive and are saved. "He has satisfied the claims of the law, and my only hope is found in looking to Him as my substitute and surety, who obeyed the law perfectly for me" *(Selected Messages,* book 1, p. 396).

Christ's righteousness saves us, but it is His death that makes this gift possible. Peter stated it well: "His own self bare our sins in his own body on the tree, that we, being dead to sins, should live unto righteousness" (1 Peter 2:24).

In chapters 14-17 of John's Gospel, we find Jesus' last will and testament. By the terms of this document, we are to be provided with unity (John 17:21), peace (John 14:27), joy (John 17:13), productivity (John 15:8), and very important, sanctification (John 17:19). But if Christ had not died, none of this would have been available. Only by the death of the testator can the provisions of a will be made available.

The apostle explained it this way: "In the case of a will, it is necessary to prove the death of the one who made it, because a will is in force only when somebody has died; it never takes effect while the one who made it is living" (Heb. 9:16, 17, NIV).

As His righteous life made His death acceptable to God, so did His righteous death make His life available to us.

As was emphasized before, God hates sin—and on the cross Jesus became the object of His wrath against it. With His arms stretched out and His manly chest bared, Christ took the thunderbolts of God's wrath against transgression that had been reserved for us. "He was treated as we deserve, in order that we might be treated as He deserves" *(Testimonies,* vol. 8, p. 208). Christ took our blows, bore our sorrows, and transported our griefs, and He bore this great burden nobly, heroically, victoriously, triumphantly, for His lost creation.

As our Surety, Christ's agreement with the Father is "My life for their freedom!" As our Sin Bearer, His agreement with us is "Your sins for My robe," "Your filthy garments for My clean cloak," "Your ugliness for My beauty," "Your imperfection for My absolute righteousness," "Your works for My gifts."

"My sins for His righteousness? Unbelievable!" shouts our incredulous humanity.

"Ah, but true!" responds our working faith as it grasps the nail-scarred hands of our Hero, our Champion, our Deliverer, our Elder Brother, the Captain of our souls.

Christ is our righteous sin bearer.

CHAPTER 17

CHRIST OUR RIGHTEOUS SURETY

"For the law made nothing perfect, but the bringing in of a better hope did; by the which we draw nigh unto God. And inasmuch as not without an oath he was made priest: . . . by so much was Jesus made a surety of a better testament" (Heb. 7:19-22).

A surety is a guarantor or cosigner, an individual who pledges to pay another's debt in case the principal debtor, through unfaithfulness or poverty or unwillingness, does not do so. Jesus is our righteous surety.

The role of the surety is dramatically illustrated by Judah's plea to Jacob that Benjamin be allowed to accompany his brothers on their return to Egypt. His words were: "Send the lad with me . . . that we may live, and not die, both we, and thou, and also our little ones. I will be surety for him; of my hand shalt thou require him" (Gen. 43:8, 9).

Jesus' service as our surety began at the scene of the original crime, in the Garden of Eden. That is when our debt was made, and that is when His guarantee was provided: "As soon as there was sin, there was a Saviour. . . . As soon as Adam sinned, the Son of God presented Himself as surety for the human race" *(SDA Bible Commentary,* Ellen G. White Comments, vol. 1, p. 1084).

Adam and Eve were not equipped to negotiate the terms of their debt. Not even perfect humanity can atone for transgression, and certainly not the now-diseased flesh of those persons whose conditional immortality has been forfeited by sin.

That is why Jesus pleaded with His Father that He be allowed to become our surety, pledging that He would personally be responsible for the awesome debt we had incurred.

In the book *The Story of Redemption,* Ellen G. White gave a graphic description of the Father's acceptance of Christ as our surety. She contemplated the Son of God entering the bright glow of the Father's presence three times in an effort to activate His part in the plan of redemption. On each of the first two visits, He entered and departed with a heavy countenance. His third visit also began with a look of sorrow, but He exited the Father's presence with an expression of relief and contentment.

Angels gathered about Him and were told of the plan of salvation upon which He and the Father had agreed. He explained that in His visits with the Father He had pleaded that the humans not be destroyed, as was their due, and that sin's recompense be delayed until its full character was displayed (pp. 42, 43).

But this would involve several unhappy prospects: first, the unpleasant specter of 4,000 years of blight in an otherwise peaceful universe; second, the accusation of Lucifer that punishment had been arbitrarily canceled; and third, the charge of Satan that deferment of death upon the guilty human race was evidence of heaven's loss and his triumph.

Christ explained that the only way the Trinity could legitimize the Father's long-suffering attitude toward sin and sinners was the surety arrangement that He had proposed: While God waited for sin to fully manifest itself, Christ would become our guarantor; eventually He would pay our debt, but in the meantime He would be our surety.

Stunned by the implications of their Master's bold initiative, angels of light vied for the task, pleading to be allowed to take the place of their Commander.

However, they were told that the terms of our rescue would not permit one created being, not even one of a higher order, to die in place of another. Only one who was equal with the law could be a surety for those who had broken the law.

Having explained His plan to the angels, Christ then announced it in the Garden of Eden in His condemnation addressed to the serpent/Satan: "I will put enmity between thee and the woman," God said, "and between thy seed and her seed; it shall bruise thy head, and thou shalt bruise his heel" (Gen. 3:15).

The good news to humanity was accompanied with the sad but instructive institution of animal sacrifice, by which Christ's mission was foreshadowed. Each dying lamb represented our Surety's pledge.

But from one generation to another, from one century to another, from one millennium to another, while sinless worlds wondered and faithful angels dreaded, sin slowly but surely diminished the human race and the debt of sin grew larger.

And the debt remained unpaid.

Prophets of God brought instruction. Angels of God visited. Rivers of blood drained from the necks of bleating lambs and goats. Yet sin continued to define the societies of humanity.

Centuries passed as the world revolved on in seemingly endless cycles. A flood came and rearranged the face of the earth, convoluting the harmonious work of Creation, depressing fertile lands into dark valleys, lifting displaced earth into stony heights. Ageless oceans beat upon receding shorelines, chiseling new configurations of rock and sand. Kingdoms waxed and waned, new myths replaced the folklore of civilizations long forgotten, and desert winds covered over habitations of once-thriving cultures.

And then Christ came.

His birth announcement read: "Sacrifice and offering thou wouldest not, but a body hast thou prepared me: in burnt offerings and sacrifices for sin thou hast had no pleasure. Then said I, Lo, I come (in the volume of the book it is written of me,) to do thy will, O God" (Heb. 10:5-7).

The Father's credibility had been sustained during the long delay of justice by Jesus' acceptance of our culpability, by His standing as our surety. But sin had now reached its zenith, and payment was now due—in full! Nothing else could do. God would not nullify His law, but He would redirect its consequences to His Son, our surety.

However, the logistics of that effort were immense and seemingly impossible.

The penalty for sin was death, the death of one equal with the law. But Those who are equal with the law are divine, and Divinity cannot die! How, then, would the Godhead resolve this impasse?

By doing a new and wonderful thing! The divine Christ would be provided with a mortal body so that His divinity and His humanity could coexist. The God who was willing to die but could not would yoke with the men who could die but should not. The Father would accept the combination of divine willingness and human sacrifice as payment for our sins.

And that necessitated the Incarnation, the process by which Christ was reduced to humanity; in this birth He became the God-man.

Christ did not become half God and half man; He was not a mixture of human and divine, as if the two had become a single homogenized entity. He became all God and all man at the same time. He was the infinite God wrapped up in finite flesh, two natures in one body, a reality that we cannot understand but which we must accept as both an act of revelation and a fact of history.

Both natures of Christ suffered greatly.

The divine Jesus suffered the loss of heavenly status and godly privilege. He suffered the discomforts of living among the repulsive elements of a sin-cursed world. "[Christ's] holy and undefiled human nature was deeply sensitive to the disgrace of being 'numbered with the transgressors' " (Review and Herald, Nov. 20, 1883). "He suffered in proportion to the perfection of His holiness and His hatred for sin. . . . To be surrounded by human beings under the control of Satan was revolting to Him" *(The Desire of Ages,* p. 700).

And the human Jesus suffered. He suffered not only spiritual temptation and physical abuse; He suffered psychological pain and finally death itself. That is how He paid our debt.

Some sureties do not have to pay the debts for which they pledge. Some guarantors are relieved of their obligations by the newly acquired willingness or ability of the principal debtor to pay the debt.

But not in the case of the Father and the debtor human race. We did not better ourselves. Our capital decreased with time. Our situation worsened. We desperately required the payment referenced to by His cry "It is finished!"

The divine Jesus did not die at Calvary; the human Jesus died. "When Christ was crucified, it was His human nature that died. Deity did not sink and die; that would have been impossible." "The Deity did not sink under the agonizing torture of Calvary" *(SDA Bible Commentary,* Ellen G. White Comments, vol. 5, pp. 1113, 1129).

But while the human Jesus expired, there was no putrefaction of His flesh, no setting in of decay. The destructive laws of nature did not begin their act of decomposition within the cells of our crucified Surety.

It was all possible because of His righteousness. He was an innocent lamb, a faultless guarantor. The cry "Father, forgive them" came from lips that knew no guile, from a tongue that spoke no evil, from a heart that harbored no deceit, from a mind that cherished no iniquity, from a soul that bore no malice. Christ bore a character that regained for us the righteousness that Adam lost.

With His righteous blood He stamped "Paid in full" on the contract detailing our awesome debt, and the note that had been outstanding for thousands of years was canceled.

When the real sacrifice died, the symbolism of the sanctuary was no longer required. The light of the Shekinah was extinguished. The lamb on the altar escaped the grasp of the startled priest. The veil separating the Temple compartments was ripped from top to bottom. The earth was shaken violently, so violently that graves were opened and corpses cast out.

Christ, though, rested quietly in the tomb.

But on the morning of the third day, when He arose, there was an earth-rattling aftershock, and from graves opened at His death, many righteous dead came forth, the firstfruits of His deliverance.

Christ presented Himself to the brethren on the Emmaus road, to Mary, and to the disciples. Then, His work on earth accomplished, He ascended on high, accompanied by those who stood as a pledge of His labors. Angels who had wept when He left glory and who struggled to relieve Him at His crucifixion now rejoiced at the triumphant return of their Commander—our Surety.

What does this mean to you and to me?

It means, first of all, that Satan's character is fully exposed. By crucifying Christ, he revealed himself as the murderer he really is. Before Calvary, Satan often stood outside the gates of glory to harass his former colleagues, accusing them of servile, unthinking obeisance.

But following the Crucifixion, he lost his stellar audience. Angels and beings on unfallen worlds now fully understood the evil of his ways, and all doubts regarding God's justice were forever removed.

Second, God's character is now fully vindicated. He found a legitimate way to suspend the law of eternal death! Satan had said that the law of God cannot be kept, and that when broken it could not be atoned. But by Christ's righteous life, the reasonableness of the law was proved, and by His righteous death He paid the penalty for our disobedience.

Third, we learn that while we are no longer in debt to God or to the law, we are in debt nonetheless: we are in debt to Jesus! The old debt has been paid. "It is finished"! There is nothing else we can do to pay that debt, because Jesus paid it all.

But that produces the obligation that Paul spoke about when he stated: "I am debtor both to the Greeks, and to the Barbarians; both to the wise, and to the unwise. So, as much as in me is, I am ready to preach the gospel" (Rom. 1:14, 15). That is how we pay the debt. The death of Jesus was our only acceptable bond; a life of total surrender is our only reasonable response.

"As much as in me is"? That means all my talents, all my time, all my energies. It means my influence, my example, my priorities, my agendas, my schedules, my life.

It means that, captivated by the knowledge of His willing sacrifice, we will live out our days in active surrender to Christ, who paid the debt He did not owe because we owed a debt we could not pay.

Christ is our righteous surety.

CHAPTER 18

CHRIST OUR RIGHTEOUS SACRIFICE

"But this man, after he had offered one sacrifice for sins for ever, sat down on the right hand of God; from henceforth expecting till his enemies be made his footstool. For by one offering he hath perfected for ever them that are sanctified" (Heb. 10:12, 13).

A sacrifice is an offering or an act of appeasement given to a deity in an effort to procure favor and avoid impending disaster. Christ is our righteous sacrifice.

The heart, the core, the kernel, of the everlasting gospel is that the Creator died for the creature, the Potter for the clay, the Judge for the criminal, the Innocent for the guilty.

What is so amazing is not simply that the transcendent God found a way to break through the orders of creation and dwell among us. After all, God possesses infinite knowledge and power, and is capable of producing whatever kind of being He chooses.

What is so amazing is that He would suffer such violence for this race of unholy, unthankful people; that He was willing to take leave of the powers of deity and, by a "painful process, mysterious to angels as well as to men" *(SDA Bible Commentary,* Ellen G. White Comments, vol. 7, p. 915), lower Himself into the foul atmosphere of this disordered planet. Mighty God became maligned man!

That the Ruler of this universe, so endlessly vast that Planet Earth is but an atom of the whole, would die for its degenerate inhabitants displays a love that stuns our reason, staggers our imagination, challenges our faith, and captures our hearts. Indeed, as the prophet Isaiah asked, "Who can believe our report?" (Isa. 53:1).

We believe it, but we cannot truly comprehend it. We behold it, but we cannot adequately explain it.

He who made us, who fixed the laws of our existence and the consequences of our transgression, also fulfilled the terms for our recovery. Those terms featured death, a quality of death that we could not provide: a righteous death.

Christ took our place. He paid our debt on Calvary.

Thus, Isaiah could say: "It pleased the Lord to bruise him; he hath put him to grief: when thou shalt make his soul an offering for sin, he shall see his seed, he shall prolong his days, and the pleasure of the Lord shall prosper in his hand" (verse 10).

There is no tenet of the Word of God that does not spring from the perspective of Christ's sacrifice. Every fundamental is illumined by His blood. "Hanging upon the cross Christ was the gospel. . . . This is our message, our argument, our doctrine, our warning to the impenitent, our encouragement for the sorrowing, the hope for every believer" *(SDA Bible Commentary,* Ellen G. White Comments, vol. 6, p. 1113).

It is true with regard to the doctrine of the church.

God designs that we worship as a believing community. Scripture likens this worshiping organization to a virtuous woman, the bride for whom Christ, the heavenly groom, has paid the ultimate dowry—His blood. Christ's blood shapes the church's theology, defines the church's mission, legitimizes the church's ecclesiology, and provides the church's appeal to humanity.

It is true with regard to the doctrine of the law.

The blood of Christ makes the commandments honorable. The law does not save; it is "our schoolmaster" (Gal. 3:24). The law has no redemptive provisions in its outline. Yet, like few other doctrines, the law focuses Christ's sacrifice on our behalf.

How? By pointing to the quality of the life that was sacrificed on its behalf. And that sacrifice is the most convincing evidence that the law remains inviolate, as changeless as His holy character.

It is true with regard to the doctrines of spiritual gifts and stewardship.

Only in terms of the blood of Christ can the doctrines of spiritual gifts and stewardship be adequately explained. We have been redeemed by an infinite sacrifice, bought with a price: the precious blood of Jesus. The high cost of our rescue gives value to our gift and makes the dedication of our time and talents a reasonable sacrifice, allowing us to say with the apostle Paul: "For to me to live is Christ, and to die is gain" (Phil. 1:21).

Paul knew himself to have been saved from the bondage of darkness by Christ's sacrifice (Col. 1:12, 13), and it was his gratitude that motivated his service. His every thought was his Master's bidding. Service, for him, was not a matter of "hours" of Christian help, nor was stewardship the siphoning off of excess time and income. These were an obsession. Paul gave total surrender to his Saviour, all of his energy, all of his passion, all of his talents, all of his love. His fascination for the cross "was the actuating principle of his conduct; it was his motive-power. If ever his ardor . . . flagged for a moment, one glance at the cross caused him to gird up anew the loins of his mind, and press forward in the way of self-denial" *(Gospel Workers,* p. 293).

It is true with regard to the doctrine of the Sabbath.
In some respects, the Sabbath presents our clearest opportunity to highlight the sacrifice of Calvary. This is so because every Sabbath is a reminder of how our Lord's fearsome struggles with men and demons concluded with rest, appropriately timed, richly deserved.

And what an excruciating struggle Christ's life had been. "Christ gave no stinted service. He did not measure His work by hours. . . . Through weary days He toiled, and through long nights He bent in prayer. . . . There was no rest for Him between the throne in heaven and the cross" *(The Ministry of Healing,* pp. 500, 501).

But when at last it was over, they laid His battered body in the grave, and Jesus found rest.

Now, on the Sabbath, those hands that had grown weary breaking bread and straightening limbs, those lips that had become parched from long hours of speaking peace and proclaiming liberty, those eyes that had been swollen in sorrow as He wept over the conditions of His people, those feet that had become pained as they carried Him across dusty fields and through rocky mountain gorges dispensing joy, that heart that had leaped with pride when sinners confessed and burst with sorrow at their final ingratitude, now rested on the holy Sabbath day.

By that act of repose, the memorial of Creation became the sign of redemption, never to change, not even in the earth made new, when "from one new moon to another, and from one sabbath to another, all flesh [shall] come to worship before" Him (Isa. 66:23).

It is true with regard to the doctrine of the second coming of Christ.
We cannot rightly understand the Second Coming without emphasis upon Christ's first coming and the crucifixion that culminated His earthly work. We must have joy in the cross before we can have hope in the coming. It is only when we have known Jesus, the slaughtered Lamb, that we can meet Christ, the

conquering King.

The Second Coming must be taught as more than the culmination of frightening signs and the end of earthly miseries. It must be seen as the wedding of the Lamb, the opportunity, at last, for us to see Jesus and to begin an eternity of praise and study of His righteous works.

And that brings to mind the millennium. It too is anchored in Calvary. Without Christ's death, there could be no resurrection of the righteous, nor final judgments upon the wicked, when they shall be completely destroyed, leaving "neither root nor branch" (Mal. 4:1). The bleeding Lamb makes possible the annihilation of the roaring dragon at the end of his millennial vacation.

And what is true of the millennium is true of every biblical prophecy. These are not, in the first instance, mathematical verifications of the identity of the true church. They are previews of events that reinforce the credibility of Christ.

Douglas Ezell stated it well when he said of John's apocalyptic visions: "John is not interpreting the future. John is interpreting the significance of the cross . . . for the future. John is not looking at a sneak preview of history down through the corridors of time to the end; he is declaring God's revelation of the meaning of the cross-resurrection for time and history until the end" (*Revelations on Revelation: New Sounds From Old Symbols,* p. 22).

The result of such cross-centered emphasis is revival and reformation.

When we are filled with and thrilled by the scenes of Calvary—when the gospel is not simply the news of a rescue about which we read, but an act of rescue that we experience—it will shine through in our preaching, our teaching, and our living. The cross will be seen in our gestures, heard in our voices, felt in the excitement of our discussions.

When we have been overcome with the joy of salvation—with the realization that Calvary has rearranged our destinies, reversed our courses, delivered our souls—it will be impossible not to be enthused and, in turn, enthuse others.

This is the secret of making loving, tenderhearted disciples. Teaching and preaching that ignores Christ's righteous blood is chiefly responsible for the lethargy and worldliness among us. It is also primarily responsible for the legalism that renders impossible the genuine fruits of righteousness. And it is the true source of the "salvation by works" mentality that so often keeps us majoring in minors and minoring in majors, unable to discern between rules and principles or ceremony and substance.

That is why "there is not a point that needs to be dwelt upon more earnestly, repeated more frequently, or established more firmly in the minds of all than the impossibility of fallen man meriting anything by his own best good works.

Salvation is through faith in Jesus Christ alone" *(Faith and Works,* p. 19).

The cross was not a pretty instrument. Crosses were made to inspire fear and inflict pain. Splintered and crude, they were nailed together with one primary concern: to end the life of a humiliated victim.

It was on a cross that Christ died.

But His death has transformed this most ignominious of objects into life's most glorious symbol, a symbol not only for forgiveness but also of righteousness. Christ's righteous life qualified Him to die in our place; it also qualified Him to live again and to appropriate that life to us. The essence of His sacrifice is that He "was hanged upon the cross that He might be able to impart His righteousness to fallen, sinful man and thus present men to His Father in His righteous character" *(Selected Messages,* book 1, p. 341).

The words of the beautiful hymn penned by George Bennard are true:

> "In the old rugged cross,
>   Stained with blood so divine,
>   A wondrous beauty I see;
>   For 'twas on that old cross
>   Jesus suffered and died,
>   To pardon and sanctify me.
>
> So I'll cherish the old rugged cross,
>   Till my trophies at last I lay down;
>   I will cling to the old rugged cross,
>   And exchange it someday for a crown."

It was nationhood time for Israel. Hundreds of years had passed since Abraham had first received the promise of a posterity, great and innumerable, by whom all nations would be blessed. The delayed fulfillment had been necessitated by obstinacy and unbelief. Centuries of frustration had absorbed generations of disappointed hopefuls.

But now the time had come. Nine of the plagues sent on Egypt had already fallen, and the final act, death to the firstborn, was about to take place. Release from bondage was imminent. Israel would be freed, *if* they handled the matter of the blood obediently.

Their instructions, related in Exodus 12, were detailed and precise: (1) a lamb must be chosen (verse 3); (2) the lamb must be spotless (verse 5); (3) the lamb must be male (verse 5); (4) the lamb must be slain at evening (verse 6); (5)

the lamb's flesh must be eaten (verse 8); (6) the uneaten flesh must be destroyed with fire (verse 10); (7) small families should invite neighbors to share a lamb (verse 4); (8) the Passover must be observed in full dress, with their traveling shoes on and their staffs in hand (verse 11); (9) they must eat in haste (verse 11); and (10) they must dip a hyssop in the blood and sprinkle it along the side posts and high over the doorposts of all their dwellings (verses 7, 22).

The blood was not to be sprinkled randomly; strict obedience accompanied reliance upon the virtues of the sacrifice. Only those who followed the Passover procedures faithfully were delivered by the Passover blood.

Once again it is nationhood time for God's people. The Lamb has been slain. Deliverance is imminent. "Christ, our Passover lamb, has been sacrificed" (1 Cor. 5:7, NIV). All that remains for our deliverance is for us, His obedient people, to apply the saving blood to the doorposts of our institutions, our churches, our homes, our lives. By that act we can and will appease the Father's wrath and enjoy the assurance of life everlasting.

Christ is our righteous sacrifice.

WINDOWS ON HIS MEDIATION

CHAPTER 19

CHRIST OUR RIGHTEOUS SATISFACTION

"He shall see the travail of His soul, and shall be satisfied: by His knowledge shall My righteous Servant justify many; for He shall bear their iniquities" (Isa. 53:11).

A satisfaction is a settlement, the successful closure of a legal or moral demand, the acceptable resolution to alienation or dispute. Jesus is our righteous satisfaction.

The principles of justice and mercy first appear in the biblical designation of the Creator as *Elohim* (Gen. 1:1, 2), He who relates to His creatures in tenderness and long-suffering (mercy); and as *Yahweh* (Gen. 2:4, 8), He who relates to His creatures in firmness and exactitude (justice).

But this proclamation is precisely the claim that Lucifer disputed. Absolute justice and mercy cannot exist in the same being, he declared. The principles that comprise the two concepts are incompatible—they flow in opposite directions; they are, he protested, mutually exclusive.

And the sin of Adam and Eve seemed to lend credence to his charge.

Unfallen angels and inhabitants of worlds above wondered and waited for an adequate explanation. The problem must be solved.

But how? Our Creator was, it seemed, thrust into an inextricable dilemma. How could He, as justice demanded, destroy the guilty pair and yet, as mercy required, forgive them at the same time? To annihilate the pair, as the law mandated, would not be a demonstration of mercy. To waive their punishment, as grace required, would not be an act of justice. By doing either—punishing and not forgiving, or forgiving and not punishing—He would deny His declared self-description, the ability to function toward His creatures simultaneously with the qualities of both justice and mercy.

For all the 4,000 years of Old Testament history, the apparently irreconcilable dilemma was focused by the misery of human experience. Adam's descendants were not immediately destroyed, but their pitiful existence was marked by sickness, suffering, and finally death. Justice, it seemed, was God's dominant operational motif in this period.

True, there were many signs and signals of mercy, hints of forgiveness. In the rivulets of blood that streamed from the sacrifices, in the mercy seat above the ark, in the rainbow that spanned the heavens after the Flood, in the cooling by the pillow of cloud that protected Israel from the desert sun, we see glimpses of God's mercy side.

And right there in the middle of the Ten Commandments, while promising to bring justice upon the third and fourth generations of those who disobeyed, God forecast mercy to thousands who would love and keep His commandments.

But these promises notwithstanding, it is justice, not mercy, that we see dominating the pages of Old Testament life.

Justice closed the gates of Eden, setting a guard with flaming swords. Justice drowned Noah's hearers, cleansing the earth with a raging flood. Justice brought disaster to the family of Achan, the sons of Levi, the servant of Elisha. Justice kept Moses from entering Canaan and David from building the Temple of the Lord. Justice bound Samson, slew Uzzah, and caused Lot's wife to become salt. Justice drowned the armies of Pharaoh, burned the people of Sodom, and destroyed the armies of Sennacherib.

It was as if mercy were retired to heavenly places, while justice exercised unbending exactitude in the affairs of the human race.

Then Jesus came, and mercy began its rule on earth.

How dramatic was the change? Drastically different. Radically opposite. Revolutionary in character. Whereas punishment and retribution had distinguished the first four millennia of life's sad symphony, at the appearance of Christ, mercy and forgiveness became God's relational mode toward humanity.

"From His earliest years He was possessed of one purpose; He lived to bless others." "Jesus was the fountain of healing mercy for the world; and through all those secluded years at Nazareth, His life flowed out in currents of sympathy and tenderness. The aged, the sorrowing, and the sin-burdened, the children at play in their innocent joy, the little creatures of the groves, the patient beasts of burden—all were happier for His presence" *(The Desire of Ages, pp. 70, 74).*

The impulses that characterized Christ's innocent youth saw dramatic expression in His formal ministry. He taught mercy in His parables: the good Samaritan, the prodigal son, the importunate widow. He extended mercy in His miracles: the man born blind, the leprous beggars, the forlorn demoniacs. He lived mercy in His associations: the woman at the well, the woman found in adultery, and the publicans with whom He dined. He extolled mercy in His sermons: "Blessed are those who make peace" and "Forgive not seven times, but seven times seventy."

And He forcibly proclaimed mercy's virtues by carrying His hearers beyond the "an eye for an eye" and "a tooth for a tooth" ethic of former ages to the "But I say unto you" principle that His life embodied.

But the people did not want mercy; they wanted bread. They wanted healing and license and deliverance from Roman oppression, but not mercy.

Christ taught that mercy meant not only forgiveness but also obedience. Mercy had ordered, "Take up your bed and walk," but it also said, "Take up your cross and follow Me." Mercy promised, "My yoke is easy, and my burden is light" (Matt. 11:30), but it also warned, "Strait is the gate, and narrow is the way, which leadeth unto life" (Matt. 7:14).

And this they refused to accept. Their quest was materialism, not mercy; food, not forgiveness; healing, not holiness; security, not sanctification—and because they hated the message, they accosted the Messenger.

The religious leaders accused Him. The Pharisees condemned Him. His disciples forsook Him. And when He refused to fight back, they mistook His silence for softness; they interpreted His nonviolence for a lack of courage. Their fathers had chafed under justice, and now they disdained mercy, charging it with both blasphemy and sedition.

They crucified Christ. Having thoroughly degraded and humiliated Him, they nailed Him to the cross.

Satan understood clearly the meaning of these events. He had heard the promise of Genesis 3:15; he had seen the long train of bleeding lambs; he had witnessed the scenes of Bethlehem; he had heard the voice and seen the dove at the Jordan; he had suffered the defeat in the wilderness; he had watched as the lame were healed and the dead were raised. Satan knew what was at stake. He knew that the death of the sinless Jesus would be the end of his sinful regime, the reconciliation at last of unyielding justice with unblemished mercy.

So there at the cross Satan tried even harder to defeat Christ. He derided Christ's birth, insulted His manhood, falsified His motives, disparaged His authority, maligned His character, ridiculed His kingship, brutalized His body.

Then Satan belittled Christ's sacrifice; he told Him that He would never see His Father's face again, that the vast majority of humans would reject Him anyway. That is *when* Christ died. That is *why* Christ died. That is *how* Christ died. His human heart was ruptured by the sorrowful truth of our impenitence.

Ellen G. White gave clarity to that moment in this statement: "Justice and Mercy stood apart, in opposition to each other, separated by a wide gulf. The Lord our Redeemer clothed His divinity with humanity, and wrought out in behalf of man a character that was without spot or blemish. He planted His cross midway between heaven and earth, and made it the object of attraction which reached both ways, drawing both Justice and Mercy across the gulf" *(Sons and Daughters of God,* p. 243).

Thus, His cry "It is finished!" was not the benediction upon a failed venture; it was the valedictory of a mission accomplished!

It was then that "Justice moved from its exalted throne, and with all the armies of heaven approached the cross. There it saw One equal with God bearing the penalty for all injustice and sin. With perfect satisfaction Justice bowed in reverence at the cross, saying, It is enough" *(SDA Bible Commentary,* Ellen G. White Comments, vol. 7, p. 936).

"It is finished!" "It is enough!" With these shouts of triumph and satisfaction, Justice and Mercy were reconciled at Calvary. As the psalmist said so meaningfully: "Mercy and truth are met together; righteousness and peace have kissed each other" (Ps. 85:10).

The estranged principles were harmonized. The long years of doubting and waiting were over. God saw the "travail of his soul" and was satisfied (Isa. 53:11).

Now Lucifer's chief charge against the Creator has been forever disproved and his kingdom eternally doomed. Now "no sin can be committed by man for which satisfaction has not been met on Calvary" *(SDA Bible Commentary,* Ellen G. White Comments, vol. 6, p. 1071). Now God can punish sin without slighting mercy. Now He can forgive sin without forsaking justice.

But it is not only in the drama of Christ's life that justice and mercy must be seen. It is in our lives as well that we must follow Christ's example and Micah's injunction to "do justly, and to love mercy" (Micah 6:8).

Justice and mercy should be present in our *homes.* Justice dictates that our homes be orderly, law-abiding units that reflect the discipline of nature and nature's God. It requires correction of weaknesses and errors that often includes sanctions and punishments for the erring.

Sparing the rod *does* spoil the child, as our generation of lawlessness affirms. Children are especially in need of the lessons of individual accountability, of personal responsibility, and of law and order, which justice teaches.

But mercy also has its place, and it is not of lesser force where righteousness is truly sought. Mercy demands that parents recall their own youthful follies when correcting their children's. It requires that when discipline is necessitated, they reflect the wise man's dictum: "It is better to be patient than powerful. It is better to win control over yourself than over whole cities" (Prov. 16:32, TEV).

And these prerogatives must be found in our *institutions.* Justice demands that laborers be treated as persons worthy of their hire, but that all stewards be found faithful. The cynicism of employees that permits the theft of time and goods so common in present relations is not condoned by the exacting demands of justice.

But the Christian's contractual agreements also include mercy. In all of our bartering, mercy's provisions will be given, "good measure, pressed down, and shaken together, and running over" (Luke 6:38).

We recipients of Christ's righteousness possess the mercy that sees in the "other" not an adversary to be disadvantaged, but the friend whom we will treat even as we wish to be treated.

Mercy and justice should be exhibited in our schools. Students must also learn the binding claims of the law of cause and effect, that grades are earned, not given, and that discipline is the handmaiden to the development of talents and a requisite of all success. Students and parents as well must know that discipline, including expulsion for serious transgressions, is not a lack of love, but a beneficial correction of the individual and sometimes the needed protection of the environment.

But mercy is also required here. Parents must remember that "exact and impartial justice should be given to all, for the religion of Christ demands this; but it should ever be remembered that firmness and justice have a sister, which is mercy. To stand aloof from students, to treat them indifferently, to be unapproachable, harsh, and censorious, is contrary to the spirit of Christ" *(Testimonies,* vol. 4, p. 420).

And so must it be in our *churches.* Justice requires that we guard zealously our image and standards. It is an unfortunate sense of mercy that allows church membership lists to be cluttered with the names of people who have long since broken faith with God's cause. Unclogging the pipes of church membership is a painful process, but like pruning the tree, it is a prerequisite to growth.

But again that must be done in mercy. In disciplining the erring, the faithful must exercise long-suffering and charity, knowing how great and immeasurable is the love and patience of Christ, how frail is our own human condition, how easily we too are found in a fault.

The satisfaction of these twin prerogatives is all the more essential when we remember that "if we were defective in character, we could not pass the gates that mercy has opened to the obedient; for justice stands at the entrance, and demands holiness, purity, in all who would see God" *(SDA Bible Commentary,* Ellen G. White Comments, vol. 6, p. 1072).

Imagine the scene: The redeemed of earth, escorted by rejoicing angels, move through space, around constellations, by galaxies and smiling worlds, to the very gates of heaven. But as they approach the pearly gates that Mercy opens, they are halted by Justice, who gives final inspection to their qualifications.

Her conclusions? "Not worthy!" Justice's requirements are inflexible, implacable. "They cannot go in," she states, "for the wages of sin is death!"

"Yes," answers knowing Mercy, "but the gift of God brings eternal life. And what is that gift? It is the life of Jesus, unpurchased, undeserved, unearned."

"But," says Justice, "they cannot enter, for flesh and blood shall not inherit the kingdom!"

"Yes," responds Mercy, "but these mortals have put on immortality, and these corruptible ones have put on incorruption, and they have washed their robes and made them white in the blood of the Lamb!"

The point is clear: their work is done; their prerogatives satisfied. Justice and Mercy join hands and, in the person of the Son of God, lead His people into the palace of the Father, whose throne is encased in mercy and whose universe is calibrated by the standards of justice.

It is not possible to ascribe ascendance to either justice or mercy. But this much we do know: When we pray, it is for *mercy,* not justice, that we plead. We further know that since "mercy implies the imperfection of the object to which it is shown" *(Testimonies,* vol. 7, p. 264), and we are provided its privileges at the very gates of glory, we never outlive its requirements here.

We also know that the two primary symbols for Christ in the Bible are the lion and the lamb: the lion representing His justice and the lamb His mercy. We know that while Isaiah appropriately extols the day when the two shall lie down together, John emphatically states that in the glorious kingdom to come, the redeemed shall "follow the Lamb whithersoever he goeth" (Rev. 14:4).

There we shall praise Him as the author and finisher of our faith. For He shall be, as He is now, eternal Lord, mighty God, conquering Lamb, blessed Redeemer, pride of the universe, joy of our hearts.

Christ is our righteous satisfaction.

CHAPTER 20

CHRIST OUR RIGHTEOUS SUPPLICATION

"Be careful for nothing; but in every thing by prayer and supplication with thanksgiving let your requests be known unto God" (Phil. 4:6).

A supplication is an entreaty, or plea, the intense petition of someone in desperate need to one who is capable of supplying that need. Christ is our righteous supplication.

He is, of course, our lawyer, our representative, our ombudsman, but He is more than that. He is our supplication. That is to say, He not only speaks to God for us; He is literally the cry we make to God. He is our password, our invocation, our plea for mercy. It is His life that we invoke; it is His suffering, His blood, His death, to which we point. Christ is our righteous supplication.

Why do we need to make supplication to the Father?

Because we are sinners, transgressors of the law. Even in our converted state we are occupants of the sinful flesh of fallen humanity. Because God's law reaches the feelings and the motives, as well as the outward acts—the books of heaven record the sins that would have been committed had there been opportunity. Because we are condemned for both sins of commission and sins of omission. Because we are judged for every idle word and thought (Matt. 12:36). Because we all come short of the absolute righteousness of God (Rom. 3:23).

We must make supplication because we know that we have not attained, we are not worthy, we are not ready to stand the test, to receive the heavy penalty for our mistakes.

If we would enter into His joy, we must make supplication. If we would receive His acceptance and peace, we must ask God to forgive us, to give us another chance. We must petition Him to wipe out our iniquity and cleanse us from all evil. We must sue for His mercy upon our poor, undone hearts.

But we have no recompense, no leverage, no standing to warrant such consideration, except our claim of fellowship with Christ.

"No man cometh unto the Father, but by me," He said (John 14:6). "Ask what ye will, and it shall be done unto you," He promised (John 15:7). We have found all His promises to be true and all His commands enabling. Therefore, we believe His Word, we trust His assurances, and we "come boldly unto the throne of grace" (Heb. 4:16).

The need for, and value of, effective supplication is demonstrated for us in many places in the Scriptures. Solomon made supplication to the Lord for the dedication of the Temple (2 Chron. 6:19); Manasseh made supplication to the Lord for deliverance from bondage (2 Chron. 33:12, 13); Esther made supplication to the king of Persia for the safety of her people (Esther 4:8); Jeremiah made supplication before King Zedekiah for better prison conditions (Jer. 37:20); Daniel made supplication to God to restore the sanctuary, which stood desolate (Dan. 9:17).

The intensity of these petitions is precisely what our posture should be before the holy God of righteousness. We sense our finitude, our frailty; we recognize that we are lost. So to the Father we present Christ, our claim for consideration, our way of acceptance, our key to deliverance, our only hope of recovery from the Fall.

Christ is our frequent supplication.

We invoke the name of Christ continually: in times of need, in times of temptation, in times of defeat, in times of loss, in times of fear and dread. And we plead His name even in victory, rejoicing because we know that we do not deserve His goodness and that today's blessings will not atone for tomorrow's needs.

Yesterday's supplications may make it easier to invoke that name today, but they do not suffice for today. Each day, each hour, each moment, presents its own requirement for both power and praise. We know that by bitter and yet blessed experience, and we make Him our frequent supplication.

Christ is our fluent supplication.

We children of the flesh, though sons and daughters of God, do not know how to pray. From our stumbling lips and halting tongues come the jumbled expression of weakened minds and troubled spirits. Even in those moments when with praise we seek the throne of God, our language is as inadequate as our feeble nature.

We cannot speak the language of heaven. We cannot comprehend the transcendence of God. Like Isaiah, we are each "undone" and of "unclean lips," and live in the company of a "people of unclean lips" (Isa. 6:5).

Our style and rhetoric do not move God. He hears the substance of our supplications, and that substance is Jesus. We are comforted by knowing that "the prayer of the humble suppliant He presents as His own desire in that soul's behalf. Every sincere prayer is heard in heaven. It may not be fluently expressed; but if the heart is in it, it will ascend to the sanctuary where Jesus ministers, and He will present it to the Father without one awkward, stammering word" *(The Desire of Ages,* p. 667).

Christ is our fervent supplication.

The words *supplication* and *prayer* are frequently joined in biblical usage. The following are a few examples from the Old and New Testaments: "The Lord hath heard my supplication; the Lord will receive my prayer" (Ps. 6:9). "Then these men assembled, and found Daniel praying and making supplication before his God" (Dan. 6:11). "These all continued with one accord in prayer and supplication, with the women, and Mary the mother of Jesus, and with his brethren" (Acts 1:14). "Praying always with all prayer and supplication in the Spirit, and watching thereunto with all perseverance and supplication for all saints" (Eph. 6:18).

Close observation reveals, however, that while all supplications are prayers, not all prayers are supplications. Prayer most often describes conversation with God in a general albeit earnest sense. Supplication, however, always involves travail and agony of soul.

When Jacob wrestled with the angel and prevailed, Hosea said he "wept, and made supplication unto him" (Hosea 12:4). Jeremiah states that "a voice was heard upon the high places, weeping and supplications of the children of Israel: for they have perverted their way, and they have forgotten the Lord their God" (Jer. 3:21). He also reminds us that it is with "weeping, and supplications" that God's people are to follow Him, not stumbling, but in a "straight way" (Jer. 31:9).

Supplications, then, are prayers of desperation and anxious entreaty, the persistent pounding on the door of heaven. It is the squeezing of the hand of God, the clinging to the arm of the Father, by that person who feels his or her desperate need.

In our supplication, we confess in the plaintive words of the hymn "Rock of Ages":

> "Not the labors of my hands
> Can fulfill Thy law's demands;

Could my zeal no respite know,
Could my tears forever flow,
All for sin could not atone;
Thou must save, and Thou alone."

Christ is our focused supplication.

Our prayers usually involve a variety of elements: requests, praise, thanksgiving. But supplication is not a wide-ranging, broad-based call upon the treasury of heaven. It is the focused entreaty of a petitioner in desperate need of specific answers, a narrowly defined burden that has pushed aside all other thoughts, a concern that weighs so heavily that all others seem petty in comparison.

When we make supplication we identify clearly and repeatedly our concerns. We agonize with God; we lay hold on the mercy seat and will be delivered or slain in the effort.

We agonize, we plead, but we always acknowledge—even through our tears—"Thy will be done." Ever yielding to the "nevertheless" of faith, we tremblingly say, in the words of the hymn penned by Augustus M. Toplady:

"If through unruffled seas
Calmly toward heaven we sail,
With grateful hearts, O God, to Thee,
We'll own the favoring gale,

But should the surges rise,
And rest delay to come,
Blest be the sorrow, kind the storm,
Which drives us nearer home."

Christ is our fitting supplication.

It was by "one man," especially designed and created by God, that we were plunged into the nightmare of disobedience and death. It is altogether proper, therefore, that by another special Creation, the Man Christ Jesus, the unique and only Begotten of God, that we are delivered from sin and its consequences.

We point to Adam as the originator of our misery, but we point to Christ as the "author and finisher of our faith" (Heb. 12:2). That, then, is the essence of His promise that "where sin abounded, grace did much more abound" (Rom. 5:20) and of the fact that "holiness is within the reach of all who reach for it by faith, not because of their good works, but because of Christ's merits" *(SDA Bible Commentary,* Ellen G. White Comments, vol. 7, p. 908). It is also the genius of Paul's words: "Since by man came death, by man came also the resurrection from the dead" (1 Cor. 15:21).

Christ is our fragrant supplication.

Sin not only causes deformity; it is repulsive. Our natural qualities are nauseating to His undefiled being. Given our true condition, we can never hope to come into His presence; even our prayers, flowing from sinful and corrupt vessels, are an abomination.

But Jesus has found the way. He suffered unspeakable anguish and lived an irreproachable life on earth so that we might know indescribable joy and claim His unimpeachable holiness. That wonder is illumined in this statement: "As the high priest sprinkled the warm blood upon the mercy seat, while the fragrant cloud of incense ascended before God, so while we confess our sins and plead the efficacy of Christ's atoning blood, our prayers are to ascend to heaven, fragrant with the merits of our Saviour's character" *(Testimonies to Ministers,* pp. 92, 93).

But the perfume of Christ's ministry that makes our lives acceptable is not applied without our consent. We must admit its efficacy, own its virtue, claim its value, if we would benefit from its power. And "as we acknowledge before God our appreciation of Christ's merits, fragrance is given to our intercessions" *(Testimonies,* vol. 8, p. 178).

In reality, then, it is a double appeal that the Father hears. He hears His Son, our suppliant, pleading for us. But He also hears us pleading for ourselves in the name of His Son, invoking His merits on our own behalf. Thus, "as we approach God through the virtue of the Redeemer's merits, Christ places us close by His side. . . . He puts His merits, as sweet incense, in the censer in our hands, in order to encourage our petitions. He promises to hear and answer our supplications" *(ibid.,* p. 178).

But God does not reply to presumptuous prayers, to feigned entreaties. He does not sanction sin by honoring the supplications of the nonrepentant. That fact is demonstrated in the experience of Jacob, perhaps the mightiest suppliant other than the divine Suppliant Himself.

Two dynamics of Jacob's encounter that eventful night moved God to bless him. First, he repented. "Through humiliation, repentance, and self-surrender, this sinful, erring mortal prevailed with the Majesty of heaven" *(Patriarchs and Prophets,* p. 197).

Second, he persisted. "Jacob's persevering faith prevailed. He held fast the angel until he obtained the blessing he desired" *(The Story of Redemption,* p. 95).

As a consequence of his repentance and his perseverance, Jacob was blessed not only with forgiveness, but very significantly, he was "redeemed . . . from all evil" (Gen. 48:16).

Christ is our final supplication.

The ultimate statistic, wrote George Bernard Shaw, is "One out of one dies," and status and popularity are not adequate guides for the journey into nothingness that we call death. Movie stars and magnates, politicians and potentates, senators and citizens, who do not know Him die with words of bitterness, snide sarcasm, or stoic resignation to the fate that befalls them.

The infidel Voltaire wrote upon his deathbed: "I wish I had never been born." Lord Byron came to the end of life, saying: "The worm, the canker, and the grief are mine." Jay Gould, the industrial tycoon, when dying, said: "I suppose I am the most miserable man on earth." John Gay's self-written epitaph speaks well for all the disillusioned and deceived. His dying words were: "Life is a jest, and all things show it; I thought so once, and now I know it" (Roy Cecil Carter, *The Royal Way of the Cross,* p. 12).

It is always that way with people who approach Christless graves. Those who don't know Him often die ruing their birth, cursing their lot, dreading their end. Regretfully, callously, cynically, they are pried, kicking and screaming, from their hold on life.

But not God's children. They die in peace. They don't die bemoaning their fate, but speaking His promises, humming His praises, invoking His name.

How is that possible?

It is so because Jesus has taken the sting out of death, and the "sting of death is sin" (1 Cor. 15:56).

Death's ultimate power is nothingness, but its ultimate dread is meeting at justice's bar the God against whom we have transgressed. How can we filthy, despicable creatures of dust face the burning glory of His presence? How can "mortal man" be just with God?

For unrepentant sinners there is no ample reply, only the dread of judgment. But for sinners saved by grace, there is the rapturous assurance of Christ making His righteousness ours. We know that we stand guilty as accused, but we also know that we are forgiven, cleansed, and covered by His perfection, and that 2,000 years ago our David went down into the valley of Elah and overcame the giant foe, that our Samson, carrying the gates of death's prison upon his shoulders, came forth from the tomb shouting, "Victory over the grave!"

By His life, He spoiled the rule of death; by His death, He paid the penalty of death; by His resurrection, He became the conqueror of death. Now when we "walk through the valley of the shadow of death," He is with us (Ps. 23:4). He who knows the way has cleared the way. He makes our passage possible.

Christ is our righteous supplication.

CHAPTER 21

CHRIST OUR RIGHTEOUS SUMMATION

"Now of the things which we have spoken this is the sum: We have such an high priest, who is set on the right hand of the throne of the Majesty in the heavens; a minister of the sanctuary, and of the true tabernacle, which the Lord pitched, and not man" (Heb. 8:1, 2).

A summation is a cumulative act, a process or statement that indicates totality, comprehensiveness, and completion. Christ is our righteous summation.

Among the more descriptive biblical characterizations of Christ's saving grace are (1) *restoration,* which presents our plight as the loss of virtue; (2) *reconciliation,* which assumes our condition as a breach of relationship; and (3) *redemption,* which pictures our state as a loss of value.

However, the Bible's most comprehensive view of our salvation is *completion*—a concept that regards our works as totally ineffective and those of Christ as the whole, or sum, of the process.

Paul gave this summary view of redemption its clearest expression when he wrote: "Ye are complete in him, which is the head of all principality and power" (Col. 2:10).

Sin always lessens. It diminishes and renders its victim incomplete. It takes away our innocence, our peace of mind, our strength of body, our sympathy with nature, our harmony with our fellow beings. It enslaves our wills. It debases our appetites. It binds us perpetually into the casements of mental and physical disease.

Thus, when Paul wrote "Ye are complete in him," he was trumpeting the fact that through the Son, the Father has not only arrested the uncontrollable erosion caused by sin, but has restored to us the full righteousness with which we began in Eden.

Because we are innately faulty, and because "the Lord requires no less of the soul now, than He required of Adam in Paradise before he fell—perfect obedience, unblemished righteousness" *(Selected Messages,* book 1, p. 373), that gift of righteousness is our only hope.

Since absolute righteousness is still the nonnegotiable requisite for divine approval, to say that we are "complete in Him" is to say that Christ is not only the sum, but the substance of our salvation.

We are "chosen" in Him (Eph. 1:4); we have "life" in Him (2 Tim. 1:1); we have "faith" in Him (Col. 2:5); we "walk" in Him (verse 6); we are "rooted and built up" in Him (verse 7); we "rejoice" in Him (Phil. 3:1); we have "hope" in Him (1 Cor. 15:19); we have "boldness" in Him (Eph. 3:12); we have "peace" in Him (Rom. 5:1); we are "made the righteousness of God" in Him (2 Cor. 5:21).

No matter what our inherited or cultivated tendencies may be, no matter where we are along the path of Christian growth and progress, *in Him* is every nuance and particle of virtue required for eternal life.

But Paul meant more than that. He was saying not only that all of our salvation requirements are *available in Him* but also that they are *accomplished by Him*. In the former meaning, we are impressed by the scale of His capacity. In the latter, we are struck by the range of His initiative. In the former, we are impressed by His being. In the latter, we are awed by His performance.

Consider the process of salvation and note how inclusive is the participation of Christ.

First of all, whatever the time or place of our conversion experience, it was precipitated by the wooing of the Holy Spirit, who was already trying to reclaim us. We did not initiate the contact. Jesus did. Nor did we respond with innate power. Such will is not native to creatures "shapen in iniquity" (Ps. 51:5).

Rather, it was Christ who "quickened us" (Eph. 2:5) by the same Spirit, thus giving us the desire and the strength to confess our sins and to yield to His pleading.

And as we responded with "godly sorrow" (2 Cor. 7:10), Jesus applied to our sordid accounts His blood of forgiveness; we were "reconciled to God by the death of his Son" (Rom. 5:10).

That is when His Holy Spirit took up residence in our hearts (Rom. 8:9, 10) and began reproducing His life within us (Gal. 2:20). That is also when He processed our papers of adoption and claimed us as members of the heavenly family (Gal. 4:7).

Now when we sometimes err, when by thought or deed we consciously betray our newfound status or are guilty of those lapses that accrue from slackened devotion, it is through Jesus, our "advocate with the Father," that our sins and shortcomings are pardoned (1 John 2:1). And beyond all that, He supplies the energy for the continued growth whereby we develop the fruits of righteousness (John 15:4) and cover our faulty flesh with His faultless robe (Isa. 61:10). It is by His initiation that all steps of our salvation are accomplished. Jesus is the sum of it all.

Does that mean that we are robots, that we are taken over mechanically by the Holy Spirit, that Jesus does it all in spite of us?

No, that is not the case. We have a work to do. In fact, "the way of return can be gained only by hard fighting, inch by inch, every hour. . . . Its accomplishment will require toil, time, and perseverance, patience and sacrifice" *(Testimonies,* vol. 8, p. 313). We must indeed "work out [our] own salvation with fear and trembling" (Phil. 2:12).

But how can these contrasting images be reconciled? How can it be true that His role is so pervasive and yet ours so essential?

It is true because every single impulse, every bit of energy that we employ in the fight against evil, is supplied by Christ. From wooing to quickening, from surrendering to indwelling, from adoption to empowering, from forgiving to covering—all of salvation's energies originate in Him. It is all the work of Jesus. Not only does the will to resist come from Him but also the power whereby we cling as branches to the Vine and gain the nutrition that causes Christian growth.

But even as we advance in grace we are not perfectly righteous. We are at best relatively perfect, and that admits to heights that are yet unconquered, elements of self that are yet untamed. The distance between our relative perfection and God's absolute perfection is not "unoccupied territory," clean pages on which no entry has been made. It is not a "neutral nothingness" that distinguishes us from God. The distance between our relative perfection and God's absolute perfection is selfishness, pride, intemperance, poor judgment—everything that God reveals to us as we grow in grace.

As we grow in grace?

Yes, that is the meaning of Paul's encouragement "Ye are complete in him." Notice that he spoke in the present tense. It is not you *will be* complete in Him in the time of trouble. Not you *were* complete in Him when you first believed. It is you *are* complete in Him right now! You and I, struggling with all the physical compromises of our humanity, guilty of our many mistakes of omission and commission, can, by the grace of God, be "complete in him"—right now!

Our situation is aptly described in the thought that "perfection through our own good works we can never attain. The soul who sees Jesus by faith repudiates his own righteousness. He sees himself as incomplete, his repentance insufficient, his strongest faith but feebleness, his most costly sacrifice as meager, and he sinks in humility at the foot of the cross. But a voice speaks to him from the oracles of God's Word. In amazement he hears the message, 'Ye are complete in

Him' " *(Faith and Works,* p. 107).

Our salvation is already complete in Jesus Christ. He has done everything necessary to save us, and more than that, we were never more accepted or acceptable than the moment we first surrendered in belief to Him—the moment we gave up our worldly ways and said, "Jesus, I love You." Right then and there the cash register in heaven rang, His blood was applied, His robe bestowed, and we were made complete in Him.

It is true, then, that salvation is not a human achievement, but a divine contribution; not a completed goal, but a finished gift; not an accumulation of deeds, but a state of heart; not a comparison with others, but an approximation of Jesus; not a collection of victories, but an orientation toward God; not the results of a effort, but the consequences of inheritance.

But, you ask, how can it be? How can Divinity risk so much in behalf of humanity? How can God declare completeness (perfection) for people who, though in process, have not fully attained? How can He declare as accepted persons who by nature are unacceptable? How can the Godhead risk Their reputation by extending such daring grace?

The answer is threefold.

First, God does so because He accepts our sincere prayers and efforts toward spiritual maturity as perfection. That, of course, is not the absolute perfection that saves us. It is the perfection that was ascribed to such persons as Noah, who "was a just man and perfect in his generations" (Gen. 6:9); and Hezekiah, who "walked before [the Lord] in truth and with a perfect heart" (Isa. 38:3).

This is made comprehendible when we remember that while "there is no man that sinneth not" (1 Kings 8:46), "at every stage of development our life may be perfect," and "if God's purpose for us is fulfilled, there will be continual advancement" *(Christ's Object Lessons,* p. 65).

Yes, the Lord considers us as growing Christians to be perfect if He is satisfied with our development. We may have been Christians for just a short while, our understanding of spiritual things may be only partial and our faith weak, but God will still consider us perfect if we are maturing steadily through the imparted righteousness of Christ.

Second, Christ is able to take such action because the faith that He sees in us is not really ours; it is His. He sees His faith in us and honors that faith. It is ours in that we are the repositories of His love, the objects of His grace. But it is His because saving faith is of divine, not human, origin. It is "heavenly treasure" in "earthen vessels."

In this sense, Christ actually bestows an advanced application of His holiness upon us. He knows that in time the workings of faith will accomplish its goal, and He regards us as if His faith had already made us absolutely perfect. It is not really our faith in Him that gains our salvation; it is His faith "within us." It is not our hold on Him that effects our rescue; it is His grasp on us.

And all the while, the Holy Spirit "worketh in [us] both to will and to do of his good pleasure" (Phil. 2:13).

Third, God acts with such confidence because in the final analysis it is not on us that the Father focuses; it is on the righteousness of Christ's robe that covers us. And how righteous is that robe? "The life which Christ offers us [His righteousness] is more perfect, more full, and more complete than was the life which Adam forfeited by transgression" *(Signs of the Times,* June 17, 1897).

While it is true that Christ's robe of righteousness does not cover cherished sin, it does cover our sinful natures, the "unholy flesh" that we shall have until the day we are made immortal. And we are thus made "complete in Him who brings in everlasting righteousness" *(Selected Messages,* book 1, p. 396).

Christ's robe is our only path to acceptance, the only way to pass the exalted test of absolute holiness, the only solution for the fatal deficiency, fragmentation, and loss that has been wrought by sin. He is our loving restorer. He is our kind redeemer. He is our strong reconciler. And more, He is the fullness of all our requirements for holiness and everlasting life.

Christ is our righteous summation.